A Responsibility to Awe

REBECCA ELSON

A Responsibility
to Awe

Carcanet
Classics

ACKNOWLEDGEMENTS

Some of these poems have appeared in *Acumen, Decodings,
Orbis, Oxford Poetry, Poetry Chicago, The Rialto, Thumbscrew*
and *US1 Worksheets*.

The essay 'From Stones to Stars' was originally prepared for a
collection of autobiographical essays by women in science who
are alumnae of the Bunting Institute at Radcliffe College USA,
and appears here in advance of publication by kind permission
of the editors.

First published in Great Britain in 2001 by

Carcanet
Alliance House
Cross Street
Manchester M2 7AQ

This new edition published in 2018

A CIP catalogue record for this book is available
from the British Library

ISBN 978 1 78410 655 3

The publisher acknowledges financial assistance
from Arts Council England

Supported using public funding by
**ARTS COUNCIL
ENGLAND**

Contents

POEMS

Poems

l LMC clusters will probably hav
objects like the central cluster i
undergoing it. Note that violen
roduce any mass segregation. '
uster must be primordial, and
rmation processes. Violent relax
)e which depends on the initial
: young LMC clusters may prese1
Section 3.2.1.

me Scale for Close Stellar Enco

icular to the formation and dest
wait for a stellar encounter to (
elling. This is referred to as the
)r such an encounter is

$$p_0 = G(m_1 + m_2)/v_{rel}^2.$$

1sses of the two stars involved i:
ross-section. α. for such an enco

We Astronomers

We astronomers are nomads,
Merchants, circus people,
All the earth our tent.

We are industrious.
We breed enthusiasms,
Honour our responsibility to awe.

But the universe has moved a long way off.
Sometimes, I confess,
Starlight seems too sharp,

And like the moon
I bend my face to the ground,
To the small patch where each foot falls,

Before it falls,
And I forget to ask questions,
And only count things.

The Expanding Universe

How do they know, he is asking,
He is seven, maybe,
I am telling him how light
Comes to us like water,
Long red waves across the universe,
Everything, all of us,
Flying out from our origins.

And he is listening
As if I were not there,
Then walking back
Into the shadow of the chestnut,
Collecting pink blossoms
In his father's empty shoe.

When You Wish upon a Star

When you wish upon a star,
Remember the space walkers
In their big boots,
Floating between satellites
And stations,
Cracked dishes, broken wings,
Kicking up a dust
Of paint flecks,
Loose parts.

You in your dark field
Looking up,
Consider the fixed stars.

You are the falling ones,
Spending your wishes
On a lost screw
Losing height,
Incandescent for an instant
As thin air consumes it.

Girl with a Balloon

(Most of the helium in the universe was created in the Big Bang.)

From this, the universe
In its industrial age,
With all the stars lit up
Roaring, banging, spitting,
Their black ash settling
Into every form of life,

You might look back with longing
To the weightlessness, the elemental,
Of the early years.

As leaning out the window
You might see a child
Going down the road,
A red balloon,
A little bit of pure Big Bang,
Bobbing at the end of her string.

Explaining Relativity

Forget the clatter of ballistics,
The monologue of falling stones,
The sharp vectors
And the stiff numbered grids.

It's so much more a thing of pliancy, persuasion,
Where space might cup itself around a planet
Like your palm around a stone,

Where you, yourself the planet,
Caught up in some geodesic dream,
Might wake to feel it enfold your weight
And know there is, in fact, no falling.

It is this, and the existence of limits.

Let There Always Be Light

(Searching for Dark Matter)

For this we go out dark nights, searching
For the dimmest stars,
For signs of unseen things:

To weigh us down.
To stop the universe
From rushing on and on
Into its own beyond
Till it exhausts itself and lies down cold,
Its last star going out.

Whatever they turn out to be,
Let there be swarms of them,
Enough for immortality,
Always a star where we can warm ourselves.

Let there even be enough to bring it back
From its own edges,
To bring us all so close that we ignite
The bright spark of resurrection.

Dark Matter

Above a pond,
An unseen filament
Of spider's floss
Suspends a slowly
Spinning leaf.

Notte di San Giovanni

Under the giant fern of night
Mosquitoes like asteroids
Shining with sound
In the untranslatable dark

The Last Animists

They say we have woken
From a long night of magic,
Of cravings,
Fire for fire, earth for earth.
A wind springs up.
The birds stir in the dovecotes.
It is so clear in this cold light
That the firmament turns without music,
That when the stars forge
The atoms of our being
No smith sweats in the labour.

Day dawns.
The chill of reason seeps
Into the bones of matter
But matter is unknowing.
Mathematics sinks its perfect teeth
Into the flesh of space
But space is unfeeling.

We say the dreams of night
Are within us
As blood within flesh
As spirit within substance
As the oneness of things
As from a dust of pigeons
The white light of wings.

Inventing Zero

First it was lines in the sand,
The tangents, intersections,
Things that never met,
And you with your big stick,
Calling it geometry,

Then numbers, counting
One and two, until
A wind blew up
And everything was gone,
Blank to the horizon.

Less than two for me
But cunning you,
You found a whole new
Starting point:

Let it have properties,
And power
To make things infinite,
Or nothing,
Or simply hold a space.

Theories of Everything

(Where the lecturer's shirt matches the painting on the wall)

He stands there speaking without love
Of theories where, in the democracy
Of this universe, or that,
There could be legislators
Who ordain trajectories for falling bodies,
Where all things must be dreamed with indifference,
And purpose is a momentary silhouette
Backlit by a blue anthropic flash,
A storm on some horizon.

But even the painting on the wall behind,
Itself an accident of shattered symmetries,
Is only half eclipsed by his transparencies
Of hierarchy and order,
And the history of thought.

And what he cannot see is this:
Himself projected next to his projections
Where the colours from the painting
Have spilled onto his shirt,
Their motion stilled into a rigorous
Design of lines and light.

Aberration

The Hubble Space Telescope before repair.

The way they tell it
All the stars have wings
The sky so full of wings
There is no sky
And just for a moment
You forget
The error and the crimped
Paths of light
And you see it
The immense migration
And you hear the rush
The beating

Carnal Knowledge

Having picked the final datum
From the universe
And fixed it in its column,
Named the causes of infinity,
Performed the calculus
Of the imaginary i, it seems

The body aches
To come too,
To the light,
Transmit the grace of gravity,
Express in its own algebra
The symmetries of awe and fear,
The shudder up the spine,
The knowing passing like a cool wind
That leaves the nape hairs leaping.

Constellations

Imagine they were not minor gods
Mounted in eternal *in memoriam*
Or even animals, however savage,
Pinned like specimens upon the sky.

Imagine they were lambada dancers
Practising their slow seductions
On the manifolds of space.

Then in the name of science
We might ride their studded thighs
To the edge of our hypotheses,
Discover there the real constants
Of the universe:

The quick pulse,
The long look,
The one natural law.

What if There Were No Moon?

There would be no months
A still sea
No spring tides
No bright nights
Occultations of the stars
No face
No moon songs
Terror of eclipse
No place to stand
And watch the Earth rise.

Observing

At the zenith of the night,
Becalmed near sleep
In your dark blind of dome,
You hear it move.

And looking up
It's there, so close
You could reach
And run your hand
Across its belly

Feel its vestigial heat,
Its long, slow curves,
Each bright nipple
Where some planet sucks

Some Thoughts about the Ocean and the Universe

If the ocean is like the universe
Then waves are stars.

If space is like the ocean,
Then matter is the waves,
Dictating the rise and fall
Of floating things.

If being is like ocean
We are waves,
Swelling, travelling, breaking
On some shore.

If ocean is like universe then waves
Are the dark wells of gravity
Where stars will grow.

All waves run shorewards
But there is no centre to the ocean
Where they all arise.

Two Nuns, Lido Azzurro, September

This is the season when the nuns
Come down to walk along the beach,
In pairs, like rare white wading birds,
Their wimples whipping in the wind.

Only their shoes shed,
They hoist their habits
Up above their knees
And walk into the waves.

But if God is this turquoise jewel of sea,
Wouldn't he want to take them in unwrapped?
Let them feel the lightness of their limbs,
Their buoyant breasts?

Olduvai Song Line

Here our ancestors are sung
Through labouring lips,
A tunnel of loins, stretching
Hot and long to this dry gorge
Where some are rising still
To score the surface
With their bones.

Poem for my Father

That was the story of your life:
Three older sisters
Stuffing handkerchiefs into your mouth
To shut you up,
Two fickle daughters,
One cross wife,
Blaming you for scandals in Parliament,
For snowstorms in May.

You kept so quiet all those years,
Tracing the earth's scarps and varves,
And shifting shores,
Calculating the millennia of waves
Rolling the bleached pebbles round,
Knuckle bones of a fossil sea.

If I could have been a son, I was,
Understanding beach as you did:
Prairie grasses lapping at a ridge of gravel,
Sand dunes in a sea of spruce,

Following you down a strand line,
On across a dry bed,
Like the first hominids,
Our footprints trailing out behind,
You honouring all my questions
With your own.

Devonian Days

That was the week it rained
As if the world thought it could begin again
In all the innocence of mud,
And we just stayed there
By the window, watching,
So aloof from our amphibious desires
That we didn't recognise
The heaviness we took to be
Dissatisfaction with the weather
To be, in fact, the memory
After buoyancy, of weight,
Of belly scraping over beach.
We didn't notice, in our restlessness,
The webbed toes twitching in our socks,
The itch of evolution,
Or its possibilities.

To Sarah's Child

... I heard the heartbeat today. It sounded like someone hammering beside the sea ...

When you come to us
From where you have been working,
There, in the sand,
By the warm, slow waves,

May we have the wisdom to receive
The ornament or tool
That you were making,
That she heard you hammering
That afternoon.

Evolution

We are survivors of immeasurable events,
Flung upon some reach of land,
Small, wet miracles without instructions,
Only the imperative of change.

Myth

What I want is a mythology so huge
That settling on its grassy bank
(Which may at first seem ordinary)
You catch sight of the frog, the stone,
The dead minnow jewelled with flies,
And remember all at once
The things you had forgotten to imagine.

Frattura Vecchia

Breaking bread beside the spring,
Yourself mute
And the village going to the mountain
Stone by stone,

A snake moves towards the water,
Mythical, precise, remote,
And you are taken by a sudden temporality,
Like water from a dry hill –

Each bit of landscape
A piece from somewhere else

Till, lying on your back
There is no mountain,
Only sky,
Only a cloud
Running

February, rue Labat

So you waited in that room,
The hours passing gently,
Ceiling speaking in a dialect of cracks,
Anemones breathing in their water,
Suggesting violet and red and pleasure:

That your solitude bear fruit,
That you invent the freedom to be free,
That in sleep your heart might press
Like some small animal against your ribs,
Towards the comfort of another pulse,

Until, exhausted with the effort of colour
Against the unreasonable neutrality of sky,
No longer with the strength to close at dusk,
They let you understand this choice:

That you can cling to your petals
Or let them go, bright and moist,
To the table, or the earth,
And so, standing naked, call that death.

Then, without shoes or map, you set out
To find, in all the world, the flower
That passes with most grace.

The Silk Road

What better market place
Along this long silk road
To spend my love than in your heart?

So go on, drink of my devotion.
Thick and salt, it swills in your gut.
I know. I too have sucked
From my camel's throat
To cross this desert.

Bedouin nights I come to you in your goat skin tent,
My gourd overflowing,
To wash your feet in my need.
The stars cannot spin wildly enough to drown me out.

By day I lose myself in the bazaars,
The bolts of cloth, the poisons, aphrodisiacs,
The soft tongued rumours.

There are rivers running deep beneath these sands,
But we lie down to roll in the dust,
Our passion clamped between our teeth
Like gold coins.

Arroyo

Compañero,
Look at you lying there,
Your sad, sinewy length.

What use was it to offer you
The tenderness of roots?

You who thirst
For the swiftness of clouds,
The quick, hard rain.

What can touch all of you
Must pass.

Moth

You cannot say
You did not know,
Those singed nights
Spinning in the dust,
One wing gone
And half your six legs spent.

But oh, that flame,
How it held you
So sweet
In the palm of its light.

Salmon Running

Who isn't driven
Up the estuaries
Of another's flesh,
Up rivers of blood,
To spawn close to the heart?

In Opposition

One moon between us,
Two seasons,
What else?
A few stars,
No wind.

In these moments
When we both walk,
How odd,
How we stand
The soles of our feet
Touching
Almost

Only the planet's breadth.

After

We are there, on the hillside,
Evening coming down.

And you begin to lean
Against some longing
Till it shifts,
The whole stone weight of it
Begins to roll,
To thunder.

And I cannot move,
I cannot make my body
Step aside.
I cannot.

And after, when the night grows still again,
I settle on my back
Saying only, *How sweet,*
That fresh crushed meadow scent,

Not saying how my heart leapt
Like the small frogs
In the tall grass
In its darkening, rushing path.

After Max Ernst

For one long day we were like that,
Our fingers pierced with heat,
Our bodies, horses, ranting
On a squall of wings,
Our hearts, what?
That caged bird in the deep wood,
One wide eye?

But that was only part of what we were.

The rest, calligraphy of the east,
No images, no pigments,
A single stroke,
The brush lifting cleanly
From the page.

Like Eels to the Sargasso Sea

It was so easy,
Each first taste of salt,
Each coming to that sea
Where our bodies break
Like light
On the surface
Still

We are not what we were
When we began
In river mud.

It seems all voyage now
Between the poles
Of love
And breeding

And something
We may never know:
Beneath us
Continents are slipping.

To the Fig Tree in the Garden

Fig, you shameless tree
You totem pole
Of buttocks, torsos, thighs
And slender midriffs
Dimpled, labial
And sweetly cleaved

Your leaves
Those symbols
Of eternal modesty
Hide nothing
But the sky

Coming of Age in Foreign Lands

Me on the shores of icy lakes,
In stands of unkempt spruce
With moss and undergrowth and no one
Singing but a whitethroat,
Where a road sign north reads home,
And spring is a month of snow.

You in a Sunday world of hot siesta streets,
A cool pineta with its stray dogs,
Old men playing cards,
And restless cousins lying about girls,
Where spring is a place on a mountain slope
Above the town,
A shepherd comes to drink.

And when the sap begins to rise,
Me in a sugar bush
Of straight backed maples, swelling buds,
And vats of syrup simmering,
Tray of drizzled snow in mittened hands,
And a Saxon soul,
That makes me swallow all the untouched white
Before I taste the sweet.

You in your grandfather's garden,
Those trees, your sisters
With their taut and slender limbs
Pouring their milk
Into the warm breasts of figs,
You, knowing with your tongue
Their fine blue skin,
Their sex,
How they swell and soften,
Like shadows,
Like sleep.

Chess Game in a Garden

Under the breath of roses
We lie
In a summer of white words
Knotted like clouds,
I on my back
Watch a bee crawl up
Into the bonnet of a blossom,
Back my queen into a corner,
Feel the power you command
Hold me in the cool cup of its hand.

The flowers lean in on us,
Touch us.
I turn
On my stomach,
Watch the grass blades twitch,
Watch your knight leap up
Tap down
Felted base on a bare board
Champing for space.

We move at angles
Guarding our strategies,
Our pawns,
Our pain,
Our claim
To a blue streak of wisdom
On a windy day.

Flying a Kite

It seems to me the kite
Has all the fun,
The view,
The weightlessness
The wind,
Ecstatic shudders,
Tail streaming out,
The urging higher,
The exhilarating dives,
And me down here,
Left holding the string.

Family Reunion

One day out we stop for lunch
In a diner in a college town
With windswept streets
Where my sister was once a small boat
With painter snapped
Drifting far off-shore.

We crowd around the little table,
She and I, our parents, and her husband,
And she holds her baby on her knee
And fills her daughter's cup with milk.

'I lived upstairs from this place once,' she says.

It stops me short.

I half remember visiting her,
Listening to records in an upstairs room.

But I was already under sail,
Out beyond the harbour's mouth,
And know so little of her days
Those years.

My sister is the anchor now
We all swing round,
Our lines long and loose.

Moored together this one week of nights,
Our gunwales bump and splinter in the dark.

Futura Vecchia, New Year's Eve

Returning, like the Earth
To the same point in space,
We go softly to the comfort of destruction,

And consume in flames
A school of fish,
A pair of hens,
A mountain poplar with its moss.

A shiver of sparks sweeps round
The dark shoulder of the Earth,
Frisson of recognition,
Preparation for another voyage,

And our own gentle bubbles
Float curious and mute
Towards the black lake
Boiling with light,
Towards the sharp night
Whistling with sound.

Eating Bouillabaisse

She sets the platter on our table:
Pool abandoned by a tide.

The silver scales of our spoons
Flash across the shallows of our bowls
Gathering the threads of flesh.

She tells us all their small fish names,
As if they once had been those words.

And we cry out like seagulls,
Scavenging them for our conversation,
Soft tongues sparring with the bones.

Radiology South

In the dim room
He adjusts the beam,
Projecting squares of light,
Like window panes,
A bit Magritte:

Blue and white flower field
Of the hospital robe,
And all my living bones.

Midwinter, Baffin Bay

How you have longed for this, exactly:
The impossibility of doing all the things
That spring up like weeds in green places.

Absence of axes,
Only proper time,
Internal dark,
Absolute space.

Just your lamp on the snow
And things becoming slower,
And more generous in their infinity.

Yet still you put your back to the pole,
Face to the solstice,
Waiting for the light.

Yosemite Valley:
Coyotes Running through a Sleeping Camp

No matter how perfectly the moonlight
Touches your high blue walls of stone,
They will always be running

Deep under the pines,
Their mad feet skimming over fallen needles,
They will come like a cloudburst
Drenching you in their sweet high sound,

And you will wake for a moment
In terror and in joy,
Their quick cult pulsing in your blood,

Then go on living.

Returning to Camp

I have gone among those rutting
Stamping wind-blown men
Out on the fields of heat.

I have felt their voices hammer
Like the stone axe,
Felt what it is to feel
That need of ligament
To arc the body as a bow,
Unsheaf the bones
And send them flying
Hard into the haunch of space.

And oh how I have loved
To let my spindle rattle
To the dry earth,
Let the soft thread snarl,
Let the grain go ungathered
And unground,
Let even the hot flame perish
In its greed.

But you, my sisters of the hearth,
Without you, there is no returning.

Hanging out his Boxer Shorts to Dry

In truth, it is a privilege to have a man,
To go with his linens to the river
Like the Pharaoh's daughters,
Like the King's maids
The day they found Odysseus
Washed up on the shore.

I love their company.
I love those days,
A warm sun,
A promising breeze,
The smooth, sprung wooden pegs,
And crisp, white boxer shorts
With two small buttons at the waist.

I love to set them sailing out
All down the garden,
My private regatta,
My flags of surrender.

Beauchamps: Renovations

I loved the space you held within your walls,
The shouldering beams,
The creepers standing out along the stones like veins,
The moist and private places,
Rare, so shy, so easily dispersed,
The shadow from a fallen tile, where a fern took root,
And high above, the sunlight
Sifting though a loose weave of wood.

When you have borne our urge to resurrect,
The sting of hammers,
Sharp sorrow of a sapling stump,
A raw crack in weathered stone;
When you've become our architecture and assemblies,
Something more ourselves than other,

Let us not forget one summer night,
The bonfire high, the old beams blazing,
How we sang and danced,
Our shadows flying on your walls,
How we lay down beside you
In a bed of straw and stars,
And listened to your close breath,
The settling of a stone,
A tile falling in the dark.

The Ballad of Just and While

Although I am about to drop,
I'll just do this before I stop.

I'll dust the stairs, put out the bin,
I'll bring the still wet washing in.

A woman's work is never done:
I'll finish something I've begun.

But one thing's not enough for me.
With 'while' I could be doing three.

And 'just's' a wedge to squeeze in more.
(Excuse me, I'll just sweep the floor.)

It's just the same at work as home.
I calculate, I write, I phone …

But things cannot go on this way.
I think I've done enough today.

Let while be something outside me:
The turning earth, the waving sea.

Let just be me upon some beach,
Just sorting pebbles within reach.

The Still Lives of Appliances

They know hours of frustration,
Cords curled, tense, along the counter,
Switches itching,
Filaments recalling heat,
Cusped blades aching
For the soft flesh of fruit.

But what eludes them
In their bursts of solitary purpose,
(Acts one might mistake for violence)
Is the recipe, the greater scheme,
The contentment of the big box
The refrigerator humming
With the secrets, the contentment
Of his cool interior.

OncoMouse, Kitchen Mouse

Mouse, whose cousins gave
Their many lives for me
Under the needle and the knife,
The awful antiseptic smells,

Whose little bodies
Manufactured murine things
That learned to fight my battle
In my blood,

Here is my kitchen.
Make it yours.
Eat all my crumbs.

I hear you down there in the dark
When your cousins in my head
Are waking up,
Whiskers stirring synapses,
Sharp tail points flicking
At the base of my skull.

Cozy up behind my fridge
But watch out for the trap,
The why-me box.

Once you've started in
It snaps you shut.

These Two Candles, Saint Pantelehm

1

Afterwards we could remember passing the taverna
With the hunters drinking in the shade,
Their dogs chained, and the smell of grilling meat,
And turning an eye to the dry hills
We wondered what they killed.
And killing seemed something separate from death,
And death seemed something geographical,
On the map, an exit point for every individual.
Sometimes you come so close to yours
You feel your body passing.

2

I saw the oil snaking down the road
And was about to warn when
Very close and very far away
I saw the tire going sideways
In a terrible distortion of motion and of time
And then a body, which was mine,
Sliding and sliding down the tarmac,
And a head flicking back, but softly,
As if a hand, arriving finally, had made a sign.
Then the motor cutting, everything still.

3

Across the empty road an olive tree
Received us in the shadow of its grace.
And all the possibilities of death
And life, and luck descended
Like a flock of swallows,
None of them coming to rest.

4

Waiting in the hour of siesta,
The hunters and their dogs gone dreaming,
The heat rising from the road,
And a kind of death, like sleep,
Passing over the unknowing town,
A beetle fell from nowhere to the pavement
With a small thud,
Lay stunned on its back for a moment,
Then began to move its legs.

5

So we came to you like that, at dusk,
To the dark space of your altar,
Touched by miracles,
Let two coins echo in the box,
And set those two small lights beside each other
To consume themselves in peace.

6

And that same night a wind came up,
You must have heard it,
Howling from a clear sky
For days and days, night after night,
Everything dancing, crazy,
Sea, stars, mountains with their dust,
The trees, the jasmine on the terrace,
Summer chairs, the dead September leaves, all flying,
And us climbing, painfully, the road above the bay.

Antidotes to Fear of Death

Sometimes as an antidote
To fear of death,
I eat the stars.

Those nights, lying on my back,
I suck them from the quenching dark
Til they are all, all inside me,
Pepper hot and sharp.

Sometimes, instead, I stir myself
Into a universe still young,
Still warm as blood:

No outer space, just space,
The light of all the not yet stars
Drifting like a bright mist,
And all of us, and everything
Already there
But unconstrained by form.

And sometimes it's enough
To lie down here on earth
Beside our long ancestral bones:

To walk across the cobble fields
Of our discarded skulls,
Each like a treasure, like a chrysalis,
Thinking: whatever left these husks
Flew off on bright wings.

Extracts from the Notebook

$$\alpha = \pi p$$

for a close encounter is then gi

$$t_{ce} = \frac{1}{\alpha n}$$

ocal number density of stars. S

$$t_{ce} = \frac{v_r^3}{\pi G^2 (m_1 }$$

v_m^2, this becomes

$$t_{ce} = 4.8 \times 10^{10} \frac{}{(m_1 + }$$

velocity v_m is in km/s, m_1 and

cluster we may assume $m_1 \approx$

a power-law IMF with slope eq

).2 $M_\odot$ and an upper mass of 0

Editorial note

Becky kept her notes in Chartwell A4 hardback volumes of 160 pages. There are four of them represented here, beginning with the first, undated, entry in Spring 1991, when she returned to England, and ending with the final entry on Monday 3 May 1999, thirteen days before she died.

She wrote in pencil, legibly and freely, drafting and redrafting poems, stories and essays. She would tackle a difficult idea again and again to clarify its expression. Among these entries, she developed the habit of making verse-notes, a discipline of observing and exploring, written at speed directly into the book. Occasionally she would draw on one of these entries to inform a poem, but most remain as they were first written – fresh, unguarded, illuminated by their own discovery. These are the majority of the pieces here.

The selection has not been an easy task. We wanted to show something of the range of her notebooks while hinting, without unnecessary duplication, at her working methods. Inevitably, there is some repetition of phrasing between the notebook and a number of the finished poems. We have included some examples of this (the barest minimum necessary) to illustrate the patterns of association and thought in the shaping process.

Apart from the very rare spelling error, no corrections have been made – except that where she used US spellings, they have been altered. Dates have also been put in, to mark the beginnings of new years. Nothing else has been tidied up, but much has been omitted.

AB, AdC 2001

Metamorphoses

And so, spreading our wings, we become night
...
 And so, flexing our toes, we become trees
And so, filling our lungs, we become ~~wind~~/light
And so, stretching our limbs, we become ~~light~~/wind
And so, rattling our bones, we become reeds/fire
And so, settling our bones, we become sleep

And waking we become all that we have loved
That spasm of remembering
                    We become the grasses of the field
                    And fear explodes in us like small pods
                    Scattering its seeds
Released ~~me from my bones~~
From the grip of toes on the cold earth
From what the fingers must endure

And having gone one thousand times to the water's edge
And found the same shells, and all of them empty

I stack my bones on an empty bench/bed
And endure, with sleep, the small emptinesses of the afternoon
...

The mind that holds itself beyond the universe that it beholds

The House of Science

Hey you! Dishevelled in the back pew
Slept all night with your temple to the earth
Ears filled with the roar of life
What are you doing here?

The room at the back of the house
The plastic dancer turning in pink
In the birthday jewellery box
You did not want
How soon we become strangers
For the first time you know yourself to be a stranger
The watermelon on the screened back porch
...

19 June

They are terrifying, these mushrooms, the way they push up
                                        overnight,
And spread, and you know they are feeding off decay,
That death is just below the surface, just, and they grow so fast
Like a cancer, I would go out into the night, as in a nightmare,
And rip them up, and scatter them, with my bare hands,
But the death would still be there.
...

19 August   [Sutton]

Digging Potatoes with my Father
Autumn again
The absolute safety, the understanding
Khaki pants & muddy workboots
Leaning into the pitchfork, and the pitted steel tines driving into
        the soil that we turned, the spring before, my sister & I, and
        dug in with sheep manure from the garden supply centre at
        Abercorn, when she was back east, & I was up north
I crouch in the earth and scoop the potatoes out as he turns the soil
                                        with his fork
Thoughts of mortality
Memories of all the autumns, the flaming trees, the apples, the
                                       woodsmoke.
...

5 October

When sleep won't come
And your whole life howls
And words dive around your head like bats
Feeding off the darkness
...

8 December

The Foundations of my Father's House

Were deep in prairie grasses, which stretched
As far as you could see
Only the church still standing
Still painted white, a sharp steeple against the blue,
And a minister in robes, black as a beetle
On a summer day
Saying where it went? / How 50 years can extinguish a town   I
                                                 couldn't hear them
As I walked the low stones
Waist deep in clover & wild barley
And sweet humming bees
Guessing at a woman I was told was my grandmother,
Who I never knew
Hanging out the white sheets in the prairie wind
The small bed of iris, gone wild
And wondering if it ever hummed with people, this place,
Or how the snow settled on it on a winter night
And whether lights burned in the windows
The bit of board walk where my father turned his tricycle wheel into
                                           the crack to stop
...
And I walk the low stones
Shoulder deep in clover & wild barley & sweet humming bees
And from where he stands watching it is only my path
         through the prairie that marks his walls.
...

1992

15 March 1992

Simulations of the Universe I

Begin with particles which could be dust
Or stars, it makes no difference
And put them in a box from which they can't escape
Except into another box which is identical
Or else another, and then
Abandon them to their trajectories
The language of encounters
The elliptic passages, hyperbolae
The magnetism of each mutual centre
When sufficient time has elapsed then
Mapping them onto the dark plane
Of probability, or space
You'll see them, so much like you saw once
Waking in mid flight, the lights below
The cities strung out across a continent in knots and filaments
So beautiful your breath rushed out
As only in the face of truth
...

28 May

This, and other paradigms
As if it were nothing but memories
Flying out from the spinning axis of existence
Mass as memories   as if mass were memories   memories were
                                                                              matter
And the further out you go, the further back, the faster they fly
We are each our own centre
Until we reach the threshold,   With our own threshold
Surface of last scattering   Missing mass and memories/most of
                                                                    them gone/
                    except one summer evening
Where I sat with my sister on my great aunt's screened back porch
Eating watermelon
The vestigial/and undifferentiated/heat

From a wicker chair from which my feet ~~cannot touch~~ have not yet
                                        reached the ground
Since there is no centre we are each our own

Where I sit with my sister
On the steps of my great aunt's screened back porch
Eating watermelon   spitting the dark seeds out into
In the vestigial undifferentiated heat   from

13 July   [Beauchamps]

The seeds we spit as dark as evening
Fireflies

Explaining Dark Matter
As if all there were, were fireflies
And from them you could infer the meadow
*As if, from fireflies, you could infer the field.
Infer the day from vestigial heat
...

26 July

Surface of last scattering
Beyond which you can't see
Earliest memories → eating watermelon on my great aunt's/Aunt
                                        Eleanor's screened back porch
Flying out from the spinning axes of existence
The further back you go, the faster they are flying away
Mass as memories   memories as matter
We are each our own centre, our own threshold
In the vestigial and undifferentiated heat
As if from fireflies, you could infer the field
...

30 August
Explaining Relativity
From Einstein: *'A Clear Explanation that anyone can understand'*
    to give: exact insight
    to require: patience and force of will
    no attention to elegance
'In this way the concept of empty space loses its meaning'
...

Figurehead

Look how she holds her shoulders
Rigid against adventure
Her breasts erect with the slap of spray
Intent on nothing
But the slow curve of the horizon

Though always in her ears
There are the murmurings
And sleeping now & then, she dreams
Of an elastic moment when, turning, she looks back
And understands, at last, the creak & snap
And the great white voices.

...

6 September

Story – With D., the time the woodpecker flew into the window &
killed itself, & I try to tell him why I'm so sad.

In the garden, hot, May, the birds are singing like crazy in the forest
all around, I am barefoot, in my pyjamas still, maybe a cup of tea, hot.
I am trying to tell him something when the bird flies into the window,
crack, and falls stunned onto the patio, its red throat thrown back in
a kind of ecstasy, in a kind of posture that says 'take me', to the sky,
to the sun, and a small drop of blood grows round at the corner of its
beak.
    For months now, it has been like this, it seems, they don't ask, and
because they don't ask, I don't talk, I ache, I am far away & silent. So

that when the tears come, which I can no longer keep back, he puts an arm around me and says, 'Don't be sad, it's only a bird,' though he himself is sad, and I say, of course it isn't the bird, and I manage to say a bit more, enough, so that later, when I pick up the bird and carry it to the edge of the woods so impenetrable there is no simple walking in, there is a kind of peace in dropping its small body into a thicket, making sure it reaches the earth, and covering it with the dead leaves that have lain all winter underneath the snow.

...

4 October

I. Evening, and the air fills with darkness,
And the darkness with wind
And the wind with moths
And the moths with motion
You are among them
And they touch you, telling you
There is no solitude we have not all passed through, or will in time
And you wonder how you came to be here
And you remember, as a child,
How, in ignorance, you left your thumbprint
In the dust of one moth's wing
And how they told you, later,
It would die.
We come as children.

...

II. Turning nightward in these domes
Our shutters opening like secrets
We set our silvered cups to catch
The fine mist of light
That settles from our chosen stars
On the edge of the unanswerable
Even here, our questions

And all of it eclipsed by the cold and catholic colours of dawn
Though we know better, seems so much more
That it has come to us
Than that we have travelled
In one still night

...

1993

24 January 1993

After the sheets and the towels are folded, and put back in the cupboard, and quiet has come again, like the dust in sunbeams, and my father has returned to his ancestors, and the sloped script of their voices, and my mother dusts away the last dry needles, and still the snow does not come. 'It rained,' the letter says, 'and the brook swelled over its banks of ice, and the next morning our little bridge was part of a dam of dead wood & rubble, 300 yards downstream.'

We are standing still, mittened, in the forest. It is snowing gently. We have carried this small construction of planks and two-by-fours down to the brook, a small brook we would certainly have played in as children. My father is hammering in nails, with great precision. Always more nails than I would have, solid, precise. Then we lift it on end, and let it fall like a drawbridge, walk, ceremoniously, across its nine foot span. Then we pad home through the snow and the descending dark, and leave my father by the brook, adjusting the branches of the trees. I am the good daughter. I am only half there.

Sarah is in the downstairs bedroom ...

We make angels in the meadow, in the snow.

We are sitting in a café on St Denis. He is drawing wings. I am nearly in tears. I am in tears. I am thinking of my childhood. How did it ever come to this? These lumps in my body that can kill?

They go on talking in the downstairs room. I listen to their voices from high up, in the sunshine, as if I had died, that is what I am imagining, that I am only a memory to them now, and my body that moves, & laughs, & sleeps, is stiff & cold somewhere in some piece of earth.

Accept everything. Accept even that, the grace of it, to be a memory, visiting like sunshine on a January day, hard, brilliant, glittering. Don't struggle against destiny. All these angels – preparation for some reincarnation?

...

February 1993   [Paris]

And all that freshly turned earth ...
The fields lying fallow, furrowed like graves
How what comes from the earth returns there.
What gives life, a furrowed field, looks so much like rows of fresh

turned graves, in this season without light, this season of mist
Then, rising above the clouds to find there is still a sun, still
    capable of heat.

And the streets full of colour, and faces, & eyes that look at you
And markets full of fruit & fish & abundance as of another time,
We forget this, we in England with our hunched shoulders,
    and our cramped step, and our few winter apples, the skin
    wrinkled, & the flesh soft.

The search for authenticity, the authentic self.
...

10 February

Consider
How the body, striding up the highest ridges of itself
Might glimpse, not the bird
But the eddies spinning off the tips of its flight
Not the snake, but the rush of air
Into the filament of empty space
Left for a moment by its passing.
...

11 February

What slips away at dawn
The beating of drums, and all this warring, these tribal dances
Along the meridians of fear, or desire
The impulse of light
And how long has it been since we saw the sun
How long since the waves stopped rolling shorewards
In the aboriginal self
All the voices, shouting, as if to say something when what is needed
                                         is silence
To finally set the tongue against the teeth
And pronounce some small thought/intention
All that freshly turned earth
And nothing growing, and no light
Nothing can make us turn aside from the truth of silence
Sitting daily before images of a universe

Where the title holds the word desire

> ...Then images
> Unclotted from the sleeping heart,
> Then sunlight and the waves
> Rolling shorewards
> In the aboriginal self,
> Then the vortex of the tongue
> Pronouncing, finally,
> Some small intention.

...

21 February In partenza, Charles de Gaulle

So much to look forward to, so many possibilities, places, people. The thing is to accept that life is an adventure, and any adventure has difficult moments. But really, it's more fear than physical. With the right strategy, the right environment, why can't I keep my body in balance with itself? No reason. Be gentle, be attentive, be understanding. Make life easy for yourself. There is a kind of joy of movement, a moment almost like flying inside yourself, soaring, with the sun, & the music, and the train moving out of Paris, leaving behind something so good, so solid to return to. I feel deeply capable of leaving you deeply free. A very beautiful moment on the train leaving Paris, of that energy which propels you through life. Places with fresh air, and sunshine, and the sea, and spring on its way.

...

6 May   [Moulin de Pique Roque]

Going into spring
Naked, with the perception of leaves
And light
No more complicated than the slip of a lizard
Over stone
How, knowing neither horizontal, nor vertical
The uninhibited leafing in the forest
And budding in the meadow
The flesh insistent
Sun falling on the pale belly

...

10 May

The thing is not to let the doctors take the poetry out of your body,
                                                                your life

La dame Picasso in the next bed
The encumbrance of flesh, too much flesh
Too much life, perhaps
'*Bon courage*', '*oh, il y en a*'
And her sister at the foot of her bed, this
Saying '*je refais ma vie*'
Saying how she lost the baby after six months
An error by a doctor
A life come only to the edge of the world
After the pain
We have no memory of pain,   only of the darkened room and
                                                                the antiseptic
Ses doigts sur mon dos, soulageants   smell and the nurses coming and
Déja je te manque   going in[to] the night
Corpo traditore, amico corpo
...

21 May

Lacework of morning
Lacework of birdsounds
Lacework of light beneath the tree

24 May

                Voyage
And you may go to the ends of the earth
And find neither comfort nor compassion
And you may fall prey to ...
All of this can happen, even
In a small boat on a summer pond

25 May

You think a river knows when it's getting near the sea?
Wide and slow & begins to taste the salt

Well I'm not like that
I still feel narrow, quick & fresh
Still somewhere in the mountains.

31 May   [Land's End]

Walking the Cornish Coast Path

I didn't believe her when she said that,
That the world is its deepest and richest
Exactly where you are, always.
Each bit of the landscape
A piece from somewhere else
The surf, and the wind
And the rabbits at sunset on the grassy bluff
And the café with one's mother's name
Eating scones, sunburnt
And no way home, we are saying
No way home
...

22 June

The Steady State Universe

Turning restlessly near sleep
The slow drip of matter
Itching the night,
You find yourself in the dream
Where you are walking endlessly
Towards a flat horizon,
Down a road with no vanishing point,
Aching for everything to be born
Screaming
Out of the dark,
For the possibility that one among us
Might contain within his flesh
The first particle of the universe,
Like a door prize
With no prize.

...

3 July   [Silvi Marina]

Two dolphins circling

A Day at the Beach

You say ...
And he says ...
By the time the shadow of the umbrella moves
And the sea goes from green to blue
Five medusas, with a purple fringe
And a squid in the bottom of the boat
Spitting ink
Two girls, sisters crouching in the waves
You remember something from your childhood
And the sun going down behind the hill
And the dolphins arcing across the light
On the water
This kind of pleasure
Drunk like waves on the sand spilling
From the sun

And the sea going blue   And the black man ~~from Africa~~
And then green   With his claret ~~glass~~ beads
And then the sky   And his loose clothes blowing
And the sea going blue   In ~~the wind off the sea~~
And blue   an African wind
And going, and going,
And you stare at the ~~underside~~ belly of the umbrella
And the waves keep coming, and coming
After the papers, and lunch
And swimming in the green
You can only have come from here, no more,
Wait, suggest something
And the sea, no longer green
And the sun going down behind a white house on a
      blue hill
And all the ~~humanity~~ bodies passing between your umbrella and the
                                                                    sea

Along the strip of shells & weeds
All of them, carrying their flesh upright at the edge of the sea
Or bent, or bending
And drinking a beer at the bar, sand between your toes

79

...

6 July   [Pescara]

And then the heat comes   If transcendence could be
White birds, flying north by moonlight
You have to seek transcendence
In the furthest part of the world
And the water going to the sand
Wave over wave
Something about the future
And the things that come in sleep
And seeking transcendence
On that strip ~~of sand~~ between the sand and water
Which is both sand and water, mercurial, bright
On the pewter sea

And the sea going green
And then blue
And blue
And the sky

In your father's house
And grandfather's garden
The olive jars
And the breadknife going to the past
And the authentic silence
And the aboriginal self

7 July

And rigour
And silence
Quantum field theory
All particles, everything, born of silence
And expressed with a kind of rigour

...

September in Turkey

3 September

– Arriving in Izmir

These are the smallest coins, he is saying, handing us three silver
coins, nothing smaller, and counting bills, three of them, or four in
the small room behind the window, counting. Outside, the bus just
leaving, it is midnight, the pavement wet with rain, though now
there is a moon, full, riding over the city, and the radio playing
something from the deep night, arabian spirit music, moaning,
notes sliding against each other, sliding. In sleep currencies become
time, tiny lire ticking quickly, with no value, just a [rhythm meter]
pace of life. In all the streets, taxi drivers doing things, waiting there,
their lights like small fires to warm themselves, in bands like gypsies,
waiting to go out into the streets, randomly, as if all this driving,
asking, might lead unexpectedly to the right street, the right door.

...

9 September

Arriving in Izmir

Standing at the counter waiting for change:
But there is nothing smaller, he is saying,
Pushing forward three silver coins,
Thousands.

Outside, the bus just leaving
Past midnight, and the pavement wet with rain,
Though now, a half moon over Izmir,
Half-built buildings
As if they were changing

But there is 'no change'
Just currencies
In sleep, becoming time
No value, just rhythm:
Tiny lire pacing the night.

Finding turquoise on the small pebble beach
Small pebble of sky
Of the sea itself, condensations of Mediterranean light
A tiny disk of turquoise, tool marked on one side, the other rough
These must have belonged to someone
A boat with treasure that tried to shelter here in a storm
Returning from Troy, could it be?
Offered now by the waves to us
Could they be mine, was I once shipwrecked here
Is the sea returning to me what is mine?
Under all that water
Lying like strangers among the rusts and greys and whites
Like someone passing speaking in a foreign tongue
Like an idea, a sudden point of understanding, that can slip away in
                                                    the next wave
Something so startling, so apart
What we lose comes back to us with patience and with time
Such tiny treasures out of a huge sea
Each like a small impulse of joy
That we have known before
Nothing like it on earth, perhaps the sea, the sky

A small bit of sky, its transparency evaporated leaving only the blue,
                                                                solid

...

<u>Parsival</u>

If one day you are ~~out~~ riding in the forest
And the universe ~~reveals itself shows~~ appears to you
Suddenly, like ~~a~~ desire
Like sunlight coming through the rain
Like a castle with a dying king
Don't ask the questions you've been taught by science
*Ask it everything ~~in your heart~~ you ever wanted

~~Are you finished? lonely? sentimental~~   Is it finished?
Are you hungry?   Is it lonely?
~~Do you suffer from headaches?~~   Does it have imaginary friends?
Are you lonely?   Does it get confused?
Do you have imaginary friends?   Forget things?
~~Was your childhood happy?~~   Does it dream?
Do you get confused?   Does it never stop moving,
                                                      like a fish?
Forget things?   Is it Afraid to die?
Do you dream?
Do you never stop moving, like a fish?   Does it have a favourite smell?
Are you afraid to die?

*What you can measure is only part of what is there

...

~~Dark Matter~~ / <u>Reflection</u>
We are Narcissus, we are all the stars,
Our attention arrested
By the miracle of self.

We are also the deep blue
Going downward
Without light.

...

Like a dolphin out of the sea
Recognition, like a friend, like a letter
Winter descends on even the villas of the rich
...

19 September

Contemplation of the Turkish coast
A beetle falling dead from the sky, like an omen
A blue and white steeple with a bell
Five hundred cupolas in winter

21 September   [Kios]

When the sun barely climbs above the horizon
And yellow leaves blow across the ground
Epic of a wind in Greece:
You, heroes blowing at the gates
Rattling the windows, billowing the lace birds
You in your small church praying
Saving small boys from snake bites
From death, from blindness
From medieval endurance
We go on walking up the dirt road
Towards the dry hills,
High above the ocean with its white waves
Asking, and the dust swirling off the road
Squinting against a low sun
The streets and shops full of the religious
In their hats, their dark and angular shoulders, their eyes
Return to life
In a hot town inland
The heat rising from the road
In the hour of the siesta
A kind of death, like sleep passing over the town
Past the bar with the hunters / have returned with their stories
Their dogs restless by the street
We turn to the dry hills asking what it is they kill there
In that landscape, as if death were something geographical
A point on the map, an x for every individual, an exit
To go out of the world

And sometimes you come so close you see it,
With your soul you see your body passing

...

26 September

Going to Samos by sea.
It is so easy to take it for granted
That the sun keeps going round the earth

The things you catch out of the corner of your eye
The things you know in the back of your mind.

Sea silver, blue
Sun climbing
Small boat passing
Through a white
Bell tower
On a hill above ~~the sea of olive terraces~~
From here, blue sun
Bright sea
Small stone church
Heat
On a ~~hillside~~, terrace, blue sea, light,
~~Small~~ stone church
Small boat passing through
A white bell tower

13 October

Falling into a black hole

If we influence the observed thing, then by observing the wave
function of the universe, we cause it to collapse in such a way that
puts the universe into a state where it can produce us. Can this be
true??

Feel the universe, how it curves.
...

Brief Explanations:

1. How science works

'*What we cannot talk about must be consigned to silence.*' Wittgenstein
   Where is this big pool of silence where everything collects?
   What does it look like?
There is a set of allowed questions, and a set way of answering them.
   Everything collapsing into words, like wave functions, an object
   chooses its value when it is named. This is an effect of the mind.
   Logic is to language as geometry is to the universe.
The reason for something is not in the state from which it emerged,
   but in the end it serves.
There is a great rift between the self and the external world. The
   self is not part of the universe to be explained.
   ...

Dark Matter

Seeing, like that, only purple
You would understand your world
From a few iris,
A few bolts of silk,
And emptiness.

And knowing the gravity of iris
You might postulate stems,
Though green were unimaginable
And seeing the silk fall in folds,
A body, though flesh could not be thought.

And speaking in purple
You might acknowledge still
The universe outside of sound.

...

23? October (Sunday)

The collapse of the Wave Function as We Know It

I suppose it occurs to everyone eventually
That simply by considering the beginning of everything,
The wave function of the Universe
We must whip it into such a state
(Our thinking being inescapably of us
And more irresistible than we imagine)
That it collapses, finally into the unique heap
From which we inevitably and necessarily
Have already emerged

...

31 October   Problems in Cosmology

> <u>Origins</u>
>
> As a flower might invent
> Some memory of the smooth
> Husk of seedhood
> So we imagine seeds of galaxies
> Shaken in the dark soil ~~soul~~ of space

In the unconscious Universe
Let there be substance
Moving neither mass nor light
Sufficient to flatten space
And curb infinity
And close itself in one

....

A summary of contemporary cosmology
...
We conceive ourselves to inhabit no special part of a Universe which
has a kind of geometry, which may be infinite, which is everywhere
the same, thinly spread substance some of which has collapsed into
points of mass which throw off light, much as abstractions collapse

into words. The vast, the dark, the unconscious universe, which is most of it, we cannot see but we suspect its presence from the way it makes things move. And everything is flying away from everything as space itself expands outward from a universal point of origin (which is by definition everywhere) in an explosion which could have been silent, there being no outside medium to transmit sound, and no listener. (Though we cannot know this, we imagine our universe to have hatched like a shark from a solitary, unguarded egg, unobserved in an ocean which we are not supposed to imagine, but cannot help it.) And since light travels at a constant speed, we can see all of this, like a memory, or think we can, by looking deep into space. We have always invented the universe in our image, animistic, ecclesiastical, mechanised, anthropic. We live now in the epoch of self-recognition. We are the dawning of the universe upon itself.

We observe the universe, predict it, calculate it, expose it to rationality, we ask it carefully phrased questions. We ask the reason for the universe, and look for the answer in the state from which it came, not the end it serves ...

1994

1 January   [Scanno]

Head full of languages
Auguries
A shrouded mountain, rain
Return to Frattura Vecchia
House full of noise and smoke
Filling the mind
Sucking at the stuff of the mind
You might run out into a wet field
Or up a plane of white snow
Wind whipping spindrift from the ridge
But no, we sit, we eat, we sleep
We are reduced to the most basic
Of what is human
In comfort still, and discomfort
From what suffocates
We walk in the dark down roads
The headlights of cars

And the lights of houses spilt in the lake
And last night eruptions of sound
Eruptions of light from the cups of houses
For the sake of another voyage, and the sun.
Does the earth feel itself to have reached
Again the same point in space?
There is no reaching a point in space.
Nothing stays the same.
Just the slow falling of snow
On the eve of anniversaries
Six months since a hot afternoon
<u>Coming like the Earth to the same</u>
<u>Point in space</u>
And finding a different season
And different people
How basic are our needs
How we come and go to a table of meat
And warm ourselves at the flames
Of burning trees.
We destroy, we destroy
We destroy to live
We live to destroy
A school of fish
A pair of hens
A pair of rabbits
A tree with its moss
Ourselves
Consumed
And the lake boiling with lights
No more dark silence
No more peace
On the television, people dying
No answers
Can we believe ourselves
To be all one?
Faces of crystal casting
The same light
Blowing bubbles in the dark
On the first day of another year
Numbered from the birth
Of this man who hangs
In effigy above our bed
These are the connections of things

The way they make signs
The way they speak
The way we discover the forms
Of bodies and faces and even birds
In the soft substance of a bone
Osso di seppia e suo spirito
To ask forgiveness for the destruction
To leave something behind
Touched by the urge to create
To climb high white mountains
To breathe, to sleep
To dream of flight
To dream

...

9 February

Faint blue galaxies
Fainter and fainter like candles,
Like fireflies in meadows
Blinking on, and extinguishing themselves
Morphological
Dreaming of a certain galaxy
A certain juxtaposition, galaxy with starburst
With companion
Star with long spikes
Ghost of a star
Itemised, categorised
All in a day's work
Amid intercontinental communiqués
Barging with our spyglass
Into this, someone's private piece of space
(And these handsome cats
Coming and going up and down the garden)
Like loud tourists
Would you look at that, spectacular
There's a beautiful galaxy in the corner of the field
With a companion
Caught in some private act
Why do we delight so in detail
Not just galaxies, but a storm of galaxies

Like snowflakes in the vortex of a streetlamp
Don't ask, just look, don't look
Saying how distant we believe these things to be

1 March   [St Louis Airport, Departure Lounge]

Knowing that you have not always
Looked beautiful in public

Thoughts on applying for an American visa:
How could they dare erect such a structure
Surmounted by a great bronze bird of prey
And ask you to wait outside the door
With arrogance and inhumility
Protecting their greed
With a show of strength,
Of rigidity, like a game of soldiers
They take themselves so seriously
Asking you to wait outside the door
No bench, only the wet stone steps
And the grey London sky
And the great bird of prey

Arriving in St Louis
And to think, this morning we were by the low Thames,
The seagulls feeding on its banks
We were by white rows of houses
With wrought railings
Where people come & go closing the door quietly
Going to work with discrete steps
And here, fluorescence, everything a strange shade
And named with self-consciousness
As if nothing could take it away
The precious flight of quick departures
From the realities of this earth
It is all for us, this is how it must be done
The neon bud sign and the television
And the cocktail bar
And the lights probe into the deepest
Layers of your face, your lines,
Your weary colour-skewed skin
And you remind yourself

You have not always
Looked beautiful in public.

...

10? April   [Palo Alto]

Weeks pass in the land of freeways, malls
Temperance of beach
And the handsome gulls with their weightlessness   The handsome,
                                                      weightless gulls
Baby Nora comes and goes in dreams
A presence in the bright air
We wake each morning to a blue sky

This was March:
        Slow walking down suburban streets
        In an unaccustomed heat
        Goose bumps from a new sun
        Smell of pine, of eucalyptus
        And nausea, another chicken roasting
        And saying this will pass,
        This too will pass
        All of this will pass

....

                    Five steps to a used car:

1. A fat blond guy in thongs
   Locked the keys in the Honda Accord
   Living with his mother, ulcers, you know
   A bit much really
   Small box by the freeway
   Left at the Seven Eleven, nowhere
   Left the lights on, ran the battery flat
   Big swaying boat of a car
   No good sign

2. Al the live butcher selling his Capri

Low, white, spoky hubcaps
Blue inside and slung back
And leaking oil expensively
Says the Turkish mechanic
Trying to sell us his own Plymouth Colt
Instead
And the Hispanics like these cars
They say.

3. A VW bug from a fat
   Lady whose mother
   In law only drove it
   To the mall

4. A Hyundai from a sincere
   Man-and-son in a too
   Clean shop/garage in a
   Place that looks like nowhere
   He looks at you wide-eyed
   Blue eyed wishing well
   Every possible aspect of life.

5. A Mazda, from a Romanian
   Immigrant with a sleepy
   Daughter, in a complex
   In San José, at least a
   Meat market full of orientals,
   A good price.

18 April   [Santa Cruz]

Dark art of life
Planting seeds, future harvests
The body numbs the mind
So much utopian
Climbing the high hill
Fog on the bay below
A boy in the high grass, drumming
What don't see [sic] is old people
Struggling, so much attention
To the blind dull stuff of happiness

And what is beyond, righteousness
And bureaucracy and hygiene
A bit unmoved these days
Contented in an impermanent way
Waiting for the body to repair
Sometimes you wonder if you
Shouldn't push harder, faster,
Or not push at all, just let.
Nothing much springs from this
Moist earth of utopia
This abundance of opportunity
And all the contented people
Wandering the streets and beaches
And the dolphins swimming up and down
And everything highlighted,
Drawing attention to itself
And people overdoing causes
Which don't concern them,
Have already been done
Singing old songs only
Or songs which sound old
Incriminating past heroes,
Procreating, too easy life
Under a hot sun,
Boy in the grass
Beating a drum
Looking out over the bay
The fog, the blue,
The harp of Monterey.

What image comes to mind
In the grey, in the blue
Weightless sky small bird
Humming at the flowers of the
Lemon tree so close you could
Grab him out of the buzzing air
Long legged wave birds
In the surf edge
Improbable legs running
And elegant beaks probing quickly
In the foam
How the water goes away
Into the sand inevitably

What is this part of life
Floating in a California house
Going to the beach
Sleeping weightless, floating
Bumping into things, but not hard
Forgot the stars, which are no closer
Look at the earth
Nature by day
Cities by night
All the interstates of our earth
And the continents rimmed
In the temperate zones
With life
And even here on Earth
*We sleep in a kind of weightlessness
Bumping gently against the stuff of dreams
Space walkers
And one small screw alone
In orbit, in freefall
And who knows, eventually
It may fall through the atmosphere
Glowing for a moment
*And someone, somewhere
*May wish on the small screw
That got away
For such is the stuff of shooting stars

...

7 May

How to poeticise the computer terminal
How science is done
One night, bumping against a kind of subjectivity
Like this: first an airport, departure lounge
Then a tram with naked women,
Pale, round fleshed, some of them wounded
Then a land where whatever you imagine happens
First, invasions, then a bolted door
Another bolt, and another, each an act of concentration
Knowing you are creating the enemy from your own terror
And that this is hell, the land of subjectivity

95

And that dreams are not things that arrange themselves
But rather, spaces that exist, like rooms, inside your mind
That you can drop into, and if you have been there before
You know where the doors are
So, grabbing three small bags of seeds
And taking off my sandals
I began to run, down and down the spiral staircase
And out onto the other plane
Of prepared beds
High above the ground.

...

Acts of Science

What we mostly do is neither so noble nor so difficult,
Making mechanical reductions of received light,
Our daily efforts rising like a dry noise,
Like so many frogs on a summer night
Picking apart the density of space
To discover, eventually, our own purpose:
More continuance than curiosity.

Always, we find ourselves at the divergence
Of two paths, travelling out.
Otherwise, our questions
Would already have been answered.

...

10 June

Can cosmology soothe the soul?
Does cosmology comfort the soul?
Two dogs running in the surf
A seal plunges from a rock
The surf never resting
A deep cave, not even shadows
Heaps of dark weed
A lost sweater
How the waves come in fingers
Playing the sand

...

20 June

Sunlight in a bamboo forest
And water, and quiet
Slow in the making these days
Climbing hills, the grass dry now
The sky blue
A long snake lying across the path
Moving as if unseen
How little time it takes them
To reclaim this hill
To the snake, only grass
No view of the bay, and the white boats
Which have become our familiars
And the air cool like spring
And perfect in a way.
...

28 June

NYT 26 April 1994

The quest begun by philosophers in ancient Greece to understand the nature of matter may have ended in Batavia III, with the discovery of evidence for the top quark, the last of twelve subatomic building blocks now believed to constitute all of the material world ...

The Twelfth Quark

Wandering the shore of inquiry,
Of faith in the irreducible,
We come upon a twelfth footprint,
Barely legible,
And feel our theories close upon themselves,
And we sit down and announce,
With the rhetoric of great discoveries,
That our journey here has ended.

> But after the pride,
> Might we not grow restless,
> Digging our own ten toes
> In the soft sand,
> Feel something missing
> From our private numerology?
>
> And dreaming a bubble chamber
> To record the tracks of lost thoughts,
> We might forget to count the waves,
> To measure each one spilling individually
> Its charge of weed and white foam,
> And consider only ocean.

...

Polytheism vs monotheism

Marigolds from Turkey, Ephesus, the temple of Artemis, going to the mosque, the old man at the public toilets, with scented water, giving us each a flower, and how seeds can spread, and what they spread.

1 July

Butterfly on a warm brick, flexing its wings
Leaf lands on a tuft of grass
Faint breeze

Walking home by moonlight through the temple of Artemis
The solitary column, piece upon piece
Then by day, the man asking us to buy his coins
The road from Ephesus
The horse with its colt
Passing us in the dying light
Big September moon, full and round, rising
Over the empty sacred space of Artemis
With her one column

2 August

Finally, some energy returning.
Days at the beach, mornings
The waves rolling in, sun biting
The ocean primordial somehow
Seething with weedbeds and
Animals, and the surfers like seals
Slippery and black and waiting
For waves
And along the rock shore
The waves coming higher than
You, filling the rock pools
Each crack a crab waiting
Just out of the sun
The anemones blossoming green
And primitive, and the seals
With their wise heads
Moving through the surface of weeds
Walking forever up and down this shore
I could sit endlessly here and
Listen to the surf repeating itself
To the horizon which swallows
You up in its enormity
To the reds and greens of the
Coast hills, how this planet
Must once have been
When the rains stopped
And the ocean had become
And there were not yet mammals
Shedding fur and gathering lice
Only smooth fins and slippery
Skins and the underwater leather
And pearly husk of shells
And the air unbroken by
Even a bird cry
Though what must the insects
Have sounded like then
With wings like ferns, towering?
How did they sing?
...

13 August

Father's Prayers for Sons & Daughters

Strange to think that even a god
Might bring himself to slit
The soft throat of a sacred ram
And then, closing his eyes
As if against the smoke,
Imagine a thousand miles away
A telephone not ringing
In a dark room.

...

30 October

Sunday morning, Mozart somewhere, a wind, and grey clouds. Black bare branches, though still there are hopeful places where yellow leaves wait to be bathed in sunlight against a black sky, and make people pause, and think of something other than their next appointment, or their last. There are still cows along the paths of the town, though the sheep have been replaced by a running track. Locomotion is the drug of these times, to make the body move quickly from place to place, as if it were all in the destination, nothing in the getting there, nothing in the journey. But all the things you pass by, leave unnoticed. So absorbed in what of the universe can be projected on your screen, you have not seen there is a plant beside you, trying to grow. We are becoming absent from this world, hardly anything touches us now, from beyond our own constructions and effluence. How we speak of 'volunteers', small emissaries from a world we have almost forgotten, these are plants which forsake the comfort of their own kind, and come to try to make us remember what else there is.

...

9 November   [Santa Monica]

Cirque du Soleil:
The man flying and turning in his cube
The singing
The two small contortionists,
Bodies melting in and out of each other
While the angel on stilts with torn, ragged wings
Looked on from the shadows
Wishing to be a small body
Knowing no limits of pliancy and balance
The clown in love with the coat
Five yellow balloons rising out of his old suitcase
The torn scraps of paper from the letter
There will always be letters
Travelling in thin envelopes with foreign stamps
Unfold me, hold me between two pairs of thumb and finger

What are we trying to say with all these curves
That we are great admirers of order and reason
That we have behaved like detectives from the start
And are presenting you with all the evidence
Avoiding always the question why
And presenting it as if we were not there
As if it just happened by itself
And would have happened the same way for
Someone else or someone else
We are anonymous, but OK how we fight to add our name to the list
What are we really looking for?

13 November

How Renoir loved his father's olive trees
Honour your grandfather's olives
And how many centuries there might have been fathers planting
                                                           olives
And grandfathers, and sons playing like goats in their grey-green
                                                            shade
Art is a way of taking joy in life
How the house would be filled with music
You, taking your grandparents to the mountains, after all the sullen
                                                             years

Grandmother praying loudly in the afternoon, and as if in answer to
                                                              her prayers
You are there, and the sun shines through all the month of
                                                      November, and
You are all in the old car, going to the mountains
Something in that high air could lift them above all their angers
And you knew that by instinct, they were suffocating themselves
With fears and resentments down there in the city
Honour above all the trees your grandfather planted there in the
                                                                garden
Where you now stand, making plans
How this chain keeps going, one link at a time, asking whether
Our bodies are strong enough at some point in our life to
Make another link, and the luck of it, that small boy playing in
The garden, and his grandfather chasing him out of the vines.
...

20 November

Wind moving the branches of the trees. Strange how warm for
November. How is it possible to take this for granted? What does it
mean? Monday morning. Wake up, dress, eat breakfast, set off on my
rattling old bicycle, through the Grafton Centre, across the common,
to the black iron footbridge where the swans are waiting to be fed,
past Castle Hill, through St Edmund's Gardens, & up to the old stone
walls of the observatory building. Put up a picture on the screen of
part of a small swarm of stars seen by a telescope that hundreds of
people, using the accumulated knowledge of thousands of thinkers,
put into orbit around our planet. Think about what it means. What
does it mean? And is it just, in the end, a discipline like anything, like
building brick walls, or balancing accounts, or sitting at an altar in a
pose of meditation? This is what I practise, practise it with compas-
sion, with honesty, with dignity, with dedication to some ideals.

13 December

And dreams coming in like storm clouds
And an orange tree bearing fruit
And rain
And a car putting into the driveway
Flying, we leave England, and the Irish coast, all green and angular
                                        with its small fields.
And some time later, there is Greenland, in a deep twilight, hexagonal
ice on a dark mat of ocean, and some few edges raised high enough
to catch the last sun offered from the south. You will never be close
enough to this land. It goes on like this, and on, all the whiteness, all
the clean cold nothingness, snow dunes, tracks of animals, maybe,
maybe nothing, mile after mile, hour after hour, broken ice & a shore,
and land, and then, a house, two houses, two small pools of light
coming out of the doors, the windows of a place where someone lives,
onto the snow which must drift and pack and squeak underfoot when
they make their way, whoever they are, from one house to the other,
and around them, nothing, for so many, many miles, nothing but snow
and the curving earth, and dreams coming in like blizzards, winds,
spindrift, building dunes, & packing and muffling, all in the darkness
[Does the moon rise in the Arctic winter?] No colours, maybe a deep
blue, stars from time to time, so far away, so very far away and cold
and bright. And what is it that draws you so, wondering who they are,
as if they were the only people on earth, the only ones, so far from all
this green. From anything that seems as if it could sustain life, and yet
life goes on, somebody's. Maybe because of the impossibility of doing
anything, of doing any of the hundreds of little things there are that
spring up like weeds in green places. There is all that space to absorb
motion, all that whiteness to absorb colour, all that twilight to absorb
light, so you could sink into stillness and obliteration, you could shout,
and all that sky would take away the sound. Nothing to bear fruit,
nothing to struggle, nothing to take shape in your hands, nothing to
be created, long long nights and the patience of all that space. Imagine
the wind at your door, the generosity of all that yellow light collecting
in a small drift, a long meditation, nothing to send ripples over your
thoughts, nothing. How would you progress in such a place, with
nothing to mark the time, the days, no clock, no calendar, an absence
of axes, absolute space, one would be moving at last in proper time,
the observer's clock, the inner clock, inner space, not stopping to
wonder about hours of the day, is it midnight, or morning, or Tuesday,
or Sunday, perhaps is it January now, or February, and when will the
light return, watching towards the south, always your back to the pole,

and one day, one inexpressible day, a small bit of red over the rim of
the snow, there for a moment and then gone, something foreign,
almost incomprehensible, you would sleep again, and wait, and find
it again, and realise with a start that it is high noon on Baffin Bay, and
one day, perhaps, a bird.

...

14 December

What you want is something more like this.
A bit of sun falling on your face.
More of this, sleeping on a sofa in a stranger's room
How quickly we move into spaces
And inhabit them, as if it really were
More a question of being than beings
Of self than selves
What is the relation between a human being and a space?

...

1995

16 February 1995

These are hard times
Wanting nights without dreams
Or dreams like roads
Saying, come this way, or this way
And across town somewhere
Someone shouting, anger, or hate
And his voice coming into my room
Through the open window
These are hard times
Asking what, really, do you want
To know from the Universe
That would make a difference
And what is a few years
A few more breakfasts
Or understanding something

And to the slow stars
How fast our lives must go
Like the blades of a fan
So fast they are invisible.

27 February

Uniform grey, cold, a rain falling from time to time
No spring, though there are daffodils gesturing
Luck for the dead in the comfort of their graves
Not going cold footed down to the shops
Returning with bread to all the cold houses of the world
Other years have passed like this
And we have almost survived another February
You must be thankful for a small room with a garden view
For friends who come and go
Yesterday we walked along a lonely dyke above the marshes
The wind coming cold off the sea
And not a thing between us and some Roman soldier
Walking there, wishing, also, for warmer times
And even a day like this, you know that the trees
Are getting ready to stun you with their leaves
And the forsythia is preparing to catch you just like sun
In the corner of your eye, though you can't see it
All the deepening roots & the swelling columns of sap
And is there something like this going on within?
Something like this, washing out of the old, the toxic,
The unnecessary.
...

28 April

Travelling light

Now like a wave   Or bagpipes starting up
Now like particles
We can only say like
Not knowing how to see
Two things as one
And asking why that speed
And not another

8 May   [Saffron Walden]

This is VE day. Here stood my mother with a glass of champagne, and so many dead ones, and sorrow, so easy to cry like that over those parted by death. And here outside is spring, a clear May sky, a bird at twilight singing his heart out. How long do birds live? And life returning even to my bones, after the half death of these months, the moments not lived, if living is to sing and dance & let your body fly through spring nights, & make love in the winter while wind rattles the windows. Live while you are still young, and be beautiful, & sparkle like diamond, like the sun on the moving ocean, because before long you will be old, if not already. And don't worry about what might happen in the future if this or that – there will be a house full of life & friends & space & music & love. J.C. going wistfully to Paris, afraid to be lonely, why is it that we need each other so, that we kill each other. Each with his curse, of loneliness, of tragedy, of self-hate, of fear. And how lucky I am to lie down each night with an angel underneath my eaves, and be folded in the warmth of his wings.

...

[7 August 1995 – 9 June 1996 is published in *Oxford Poets 2000*]

1996

Monday 10 June 1996

The sky like a firework
Stopped mid-shower
A bee causes a shower of rose petals   provokes an avalanche of
                                                        petals
Me in the row boat, not going far
Or around the meadow
Through the middle of the meadow
Connecting with something
Some joyfulness, the generosity of meadows

Be like the small lizard on the warm stone
Still, then darting, then still
The frog floating limply

Letting the green water hold it
Let the Earth hold you
And (if not the Earth), the sky

Willow spilling itself towards the green water
These have been long years
To feel again the body slipping nymph like
Through a green pond
In the company of fish, water bugs
A little panic of frogs

Wednesday 12 June

Frogs skipping themselves like stones
Across a weedy pond
...

Missing matter

Dark matter is an unseen filament of spider's floss
Suspending a slowly spinning leaf above a pond
It is the lips of a fish touching the surface
Sending out ripples
Dark matter inside us – memory, associations
It is what makes you remember something from your childhood
The damp smell of a basement,
The mothball smell of an old trunk
The brittle dusty smell of an attic
The smell of a certain herb
That makes you feel sudden sadness, sudden joy
Sweet clover, heat, a poplar breeze
Everything inside you that you cannot see, that makes you move
It is unconscious
The known human forces, love & hunger, fear and hope   faith
                                        forces of attraction
Each of us moving in the field of these forces
A unified theory of these human forces
But what these forces arise from are our dark wells of memories
Of instincts, of collective signs, of deities
All the invisible things in this world
That leave their traces

A night frost leaving blackened leaves
It is the black stuff of coal that glows orange in an ember
If an air bubble breaks the surface, sends out ripples
Then dark matter is the passing fish

...

Dark Matter II

In this, our galaxy of human ways
Each of us, point-like, luminous
Bends the path of those whose lives we touch.

But there is something more.
That keeps us circling a common centre,
Stops us spinning off into the void

You feel it in an unexpected pull
A sudden swerve of thought, mid-stride:
The deep well of almost weightless memory.
The dense body of a passing god.

...

4 September   Modena

And now, September with its rare light
A night train, rain coming down warm
On the fields outside
How completely different each from all the others
We are, how one thinks of a soft space beyond
The mechanics of our current cosmos
Where things merge & mix & lose time as an
Arrow, or more a sphere, things we can almost
Remember, a space accommodating
Only the appearance of zero, minus one and one, always
Because nothing has no sense
And the other with the power of science
The childhood of knowledge, to control all
To condemn poetry, the spirit
Because curiosity, after all, is also of the spirit,

And so is the desire to control and reduce
And rebuild according to uniform law.
Is this what I do too, with all my days
Recording the arrangements of stars
And their possible destinies
But the other senses – the sound, the smells
Where are they in this world we immerse ourselves
That we should think, not feel –
Our poems should be dismantled
Leaving bare paths, and our religions –
Our religions stripped of all their skins
As if there were explanations
The god of explanation rising supreme
Gods of the smallest particles
But explanation is not understanding
And what is understanding, does it not involve
As well the souls, & is it not itself a feeling
That moment of connecting two things, or three
That pleasure, the revolutions of the soul

7 September   Pescara

Cold, grey, rain coming slanting down,
Violin without a string, without a tune
Trees without leaves, earth without grass
Without care, without love, we live in our cement towers
Elbows on windowsills, looking out
Antiseptic, no muddy feet, no marching over fields
No cycling through winds, sad, empty, a bit lost
Like all of us, returning to work without adventure
And no one to sweeten our souls
I would say it comes to this:
Grandparents married fifty years today, & angry
Sharp & thin with hand raised as good as a curse
But kindness too, in a little breeze,
And after the suffering, the rain

Figs, the most sensuous of trees,
Their grey formings mocking the crevices
Of our own bodies, our thighs,
Our buttocks, the backs of knees
And beyond, ivy rising thick & purposeful

Thinking itself to have found its ruin
The brick wall three storeys high,
To be painting it in slow strokes of green and red.

I would like to be beside the river
Where I was as a child
Sun coming through the trees
A pool too deep & shadowy
And nothing to do but watch for fish
And come away from there and run
Over all the same paths of my lives
Climbing towards a sunlit meadow
Where finally I might rest.

Like the joy of listening to the wedding bells
And knowing they are yours
That clamour, all that joy, for you.
And walking in a bride's clothes
Through a garden in a hot sun.

Here, look, the horses, wingless
For the footless angels
The earth spinning
Under the strike   The Earth sent spinning
Of their feet   Underneath their sinking hoofs
...

11 September

Then the sun & finally the sea and, you know
The hot sand under your feet & then your belly
And a green horizon, small waves coming in
Yesterday a sea bat, a dense black mollusc
Rippling its velvet wings just below the surface
In the shallow sea, tentacled head raised upwards
And velvet to the touch. What deep pleasure
This heat, this air, this September sun
The beach abandoned, the small fish returning
This place is no longer old
No longer with its old men sitting

No longer the faces from Roman villas, from Etruscan tombs
And all women growing to the same shape

Travelling Light

Time no longer moves
But who made light move at a certain
Speed & only that, & why that
Whose idea was that?
Even light takes time to move across a room
So that as it passes, so things change
And so, looking far away, we look into the past
Even as light perceives us as inanimate
Motionless, static in our elements of air and earth
So we see other things that move more slow than us.
And so with speed things move outside our
Window of perception, like the blades of a fan
Space contracts, in its elegant rapport with time
Things are only what they seem
And nothing more
Our perceptions squeezed into a tiny space of speed and colour
Imagining all the things we cannot see
A pale, dark sun, a star too bright to look
The sky in pieces, the way the earth, with its slow ageing
Sees the stars shoot past like meteors
We too are free to see things as we choose
With patience we could watch a flower open
A mushroom push above the earth
The stars heaving and contracting, surging & fading
We carry what comforts and sustains
Which can be space itself & time
Not things, which only weigh us down
Stepping gently over the earth
If you could move like light
How things would slow, & stop

17 September

Still on the beach, still the wind fresh off the sea
But the mountains shining with snow, and untouchable
Still the sky blue to the horizon
Meeting respectfully the other blue of the sea
A fringe of little rippling waves, then honey sand
With its display of shells & sticks & lost things
And me, still here, still present in this world.
What next in life?
After the year I bought a house, and married, & was cured (I pray)
What next, what now?
Not to let the years go by unaccounted for, unnumbered

Not just here under the Universe
But in it, growing out of it
And you for whom the stars are not always out
For whom the daily chores eclipse the universe itself
Never to lose the poetry that runs through things
That you should sit with your *Repubblica*
Spread on a beach chair, the pages flipping
And curving in the breeze
On the beach where you played as a child
Only a few old men strolling along the water's edge
And a dog, probably abandoned,
Delirious with pleasure racing up & down the sand
Into the waves, barking now & then in the hope
Of a stick to chase, with pure joy
Not knowing that winter is on its way.

...

23 October

Creation
The Universe spilt And spreading Like a stain

Dark Matter – I

Above a pond
An unseen filament
Of spider's floss
Suspending a slowly
Spinning leaf

...

31 October

Dark Matter II

Like the thing you were about to say

The thing that pulls you to a certain room
And leaves you standing, mystified

Isaac & Eve

Before the Fall
Of the apple
Mutual attraction
Was not fully understood

After the Fall
Of the apple
Mutual attraction
Was better understood

28 November

Tomorrow is one of the days
I have left to live

1 December

Grey day
Damp wind in the fen
Left leaves

Sometimes the mornings light up with frost

Attention to detail
At the iron bridge
Its lattice sides
Each with a spider's web
And sometimes, each strand
Beaded with dew
And sometimes ice crystals
Beading each and every strand

...

Riding to Work

1. Cemetery – puddled path, leaning stones,
    Sometimes berries, sometimes birds
    This film of broken ice
    A bench, a person with a dog
    And open iron gate

2. Grafton Centre
    All the sellers showing all their things
    Stop at the red letter box
    Cheerful cylinder, like something for a child
    And the postmen on their bicycles, like boys

3. Across the green, the common
    Through the tunnel of plane trees
    Slanting light, leaves papering the grass

4. Crossing the river, there the iron footbridge
    There by the paved stepped bank a man
    A child, feeding bread to the ducks, to swans
    Maybe a mist, maybe a spiderweb in every
    Lattice diamond, beaded with mist

5. St Edmund's apples
    Like small yellow lanterns
    On a leafless tree

23 December   [Anstruther]

Here the sea again rolling and rolling
The never silent sea, that could suddenly be split
Into stillness and silence
Sun rising late, rising all day long until it sets
Sun somewhere else and here all day the orange clouds
And us on a black topped heather mountain
Springing down a long slope, ducking our heads beneath
The ceiling clouds scudding up to mountains
Lit by snow and shining, magic totems you must hold
And blow on till they melt & fade green again
We stand above the harbour, we listen to the waves

Small shop in Falkland
Man in an armchair sketching a trophy from a postcard
White hair, earring, and all around him, violins
Two transparent ones made in 1956 by a man in Kirkcaldy
From the perspex cockpit of a Spitfire crashed in town.

...

1997

9 February 1997

Home from college, the summer before it all changed
Working two jobs, one an office
Sitting by a phone that never rang
A novel open in the top desk drawer
The other, nights, a cigarette shop
Men coming in, their cars idling outside
How young I must have looked
About to go to Europe for a year
Waiting for closing time
The sweet tobacco smell
Leafing through a *Playboy*
Eating smarties, one from each box

Scotland at Christmas

Sun rising all day long, rising
Till it sets
Spring down a hillside on black heather
Head ducking under clouds
And down there, snowcapped mountains
Shining totems you might hold
And blow on till they melt

...

24 February

February day

The teasing yellow /colours/ of the crocuses
Scattered like Easter eggs across the lawn
The grey, the wind
The dripping of the gutters on the pavement
Underneath your window
All night, moonless night
Month too short to grow a moon
The fire sparking like magicians
What matters now is what goes on
In the reefs of your bones
In the oceans of your flesh
What whales are bellowing across your blood
Heart thrumming like an ocean liner
What small fish are pecking at the coral reef of your bones
What strange colonies are flourishing
What transparent creatures run along your nerves
Rising like bubbles from the hot vents of creation   from your deep

...

28 February

Crossing

What touched me
Diving through the currents
Of your blood,
The clouds of red and pale plankton,
Coral reefs of bone,

Was not your deepest, blackest canyons,
Not the vents, the alchemy,
The strange, transparent, half-thought things,

But the thrumming of your ceaseless,
Your disturbing heart:
That untried ocean liner
On its maiden –
On its only –
Voyage

February gone now, for another year
The wind dropped, the bravest flowers unfolding
What will summer bring. Don't ask.
If pleasure, suffering, don't ask
So many plans & projects, so many things still to do.
...
Poem for my Father's Seventieth Birthday

Letters from the past
Too much living in the adventures of another's life
An ancestor, a way of trying to be there
Always in a woman's world
Of elder sisters, wife, & daughters
Shrewish, moody, cross, demanding
Always scolded, never left to be,
To clatter, play the trombone
Like an elephant stampeding through the basement

Telling stories, gentle with the chickadeeds, [*sic*]
The jays, and always watching,
Measuring, the natural world:
    The way a mushroom grows
    The way frost heaves
    A moonscape erodes
    A green plant shrinks
    The temperature goes up and down beneath the roof
    Your daughters grow
Capturing snowflakes on the driveway
On a black velvet cloth
And keeping them, like magicians.
...

7 May

I was born in the coldest hour of the night
At four in the morning in a blizzard
At the time of the year when the earth comes closest to the sun
On the second day of the decade of free love
And walking on the moon.

There was my sister, fourteen months already in the world
My mother, a sensible age I would think it now, for children,
Having already worked & lived & been in Paris at the end of the war
And my father, a professor in a sunny study with geraniums and maps

My grandmother came from time to time
On something called a train from somewhere far away
Wearing dark dresses with cloth whose patterns I could see
    long after I pressed my hands hard against my eyes.
And Daisy who taught us to curtsey & soften butter
    by holding it on a knife above a steaming bowl of soup,
    and once stood by my bed
in the dark on New Year's Eve, holding a radio
to my ear, a bell striking faintly midnight, though it /wasn't my
                                        bedtime/

wasn't yet, & telling me it was Big Ben
(brought enormous copper pennies)

10 May

In the summer, every summer, we were gone
Out west, up north
Measuring stick, sample bag, tent
Blue hooded jackets, mosquito repellent
Smelling of canvas tents & mosquito repellent & sweet clover
Lakes in the woods, lakes in the prairies
Cotton fluff trees, poplars, pines
Mud, minnows, pebbles,
Me in a canvas tent bag jumping across a field of thistles

Winter snow, walking to school in big boots
Pushing cars out of snowdrifts
Long winter nights & Christmas   skating, tobogganing, boys

Went on a trip with my mother, south
To colleges with green campuses, red leaves
To choose, to go away
Bands playing, crowds of young people
Bus rides at night
Snow falling on the quadrangle
China with small flowers, and dancing

Third year we went abroad, me & Mary
To a tiny Scottish town, cathedral ruins
Castle ruins, west sands, east sands, fishing harbour
Cold sea licking & sucking, rain, all-day sunsets.

Come Christmas we got a train to Europe, we did
Weighed down with things, cold in stations
Sleeping, waiting, everyone else at home, and us
Adventurers reading our maps, & trying to be brave
In Monte Carlo, and Florence at dawn dozing on a pew in a cold
church
Drinking coffee from tiny cups, Rome, Munich, Salzburg,
Paris, sheets of grey ice under the Eiffel Tower,
And north again.

Then in that town I fell in love,
First time, laying my head on the soft shoulder of hills
The wind shaking the tent like a dust cloth

All night long, and the aurora rising from a ridge
I stayed a summer, and another
Working in a room of grey metal shelving
Scanning the universe, looking for certain things.

But the second one was different. It rained
Love washed away. Friendship wasn't good enough.
I was going down another road.

I went back to Canada, way out west
Finding myself my first house
Five of us, one on his elbow on the sofa
Smoking or chewing toothpicks, loud jazz
One plump & lazy & smart.
One slick, British, little sack of hash in a zipped up boot, shades,
One a good girl, studious & kind.

I fell in love again.
I solved equations. It rained.
We climbed mountains, and those were the best days
Coming down in the dark, looking for the shiny blaze nailed on
trees
To mark the way, exhausted, aching
Full of mountains
It rained. Love moved in and out.
No friends, just men, and me in the basement, crying and alone.

I got away, it felt like that
Selling the bike I had since I was twelve
The twelve string guitar I paid for with a case of beer
I went one way, him the other
But we kept friends. Fifteen years that was.
He was here last week.

Came back to England, autumn,
New in town, smells of coal smoke, beer.
It rained, & I took on a galaxy
A certain one, the nearest one, not to feel
Too far away, too cold.

The phone rang.
My grandmother had died.

Easter came. And Mary. And when she left
I fell in love again, and this time deep & hard
Letting go of all the handholds
All the chocks unzipping
It was ten years till I hit the ground
Though there were bumps along the way
And sometimes a catch on a thin ledge
And what a view – to convince yourself
It's worth the fall. It was.

Meanwhile, they sent me south, to Australia
Hot nights, gum tree scented
My galaxy spinning overhead
Walking down a valley, down a dusty road
Waiting for letters from Italy.

They sent me to Baltimore, mid winter
Squirrels falling frozen out of trees
My lover a small bottle of olive oil, cloudy thick
Waiting for phone calls
Flying to Italy
Him, the other woman (me), his wife.
And no one learning much.

I thrashed it through. I wrote a thesis.
I said I didn't care
But when the time came to receive that last degree
To move out of studenthood for good
He was there again declaring endless love
Me, the other woman, she the wife, our man.

I went away. I said goodbye. I went.
To an east coast autumn. That at least I loved.
My own apartment, all one room
And all around me, mathematics, stars.
No one to tell stories, sing songs
No one lighted by that land of life.

Another man came with darkness and fury
And I was swept away, but found
The lease on my heart wasn't up.
I found the lumps, I fingered them
And lay awake at night.

They cut one out. I waited.
Fear, all fear, no pain, still
Though I have cut my feet on sharp stones
And crossed high bridges over black water
And been chased and bitten by sharp toothed animals.

I went back, to my England, the house,
The sisters by adoption
The garden with its head high summer poppies
And its winter rain.
I hit the ground, and landed lightly in the end
With springs of anger on my feet
Bouncing from Australia, feeling finally
Free of falling.

I went alone to the cinema on Sunday afternoons
I didn't have to talk to anyone
I tossed out all my arms & legs the full stretch of bed.
I wrote.

And when the time was right I wrote a postcard
To a man I knew in Paris
Had known through all the falling
Would not have known without it
And we met like that in a different way
Sleeping under the stars by the embers of a bonfire.

11 May

Science is not what they say, so serious
The truth being what you imagine
Not what you see
And not something useful
Or something that pays

18 May

Like following a small thread
Out and out and out
What catches at your core
How many times you can plant
In the same earth
How many more summer nights
To wait at the window
For that warm rain
And how quick the flowers fade
How many conversations
Passing under the window

...

September [Ischia]

Lunar Eclipse

High noon on the moon:
The huge blue round of earth
Slides across the yellow sun.

Down here, above the table of Capri
Dusk and a full white moon goes smoky red and dim,
Long shadows streaming into space
Snuff out the shimmer on the sea.

...

23 November

Sutton in October

'Mon pays ce n'est pas un pays, c'est l'hiver'

Going up into the forest after a snowfall
I climb away from the house
Stand still, so still the only sound
My pulse in my ears
A branch creaking in a high up wind
It comes to me that
Though I cannot recall generations in this place

And am a seed that blew here from somewhere else
Made shallow roots, & grew a bit, & moved on,
That whenever I found myself, if it looked like this,
The quiet grey poles of trees,
The snow smoothing and silencing everything
The cold in my lungs making my blood race
It would feel like home.

Opening boxes in the basement
All the little things that belong to me

30 November

Sutton in October
How families can be fragmented and together

I go down to the brook
Which is tiled now with fallen leaves
Which runs cold over the smooth stones
And think of all the brooks where I have sat
And the comfort in a brook
The way the water keeps coming
Keeps singing

I shovel away at a big pile of earth,
Duck manure & woodchips
With my father, methodical
For five years I have not been here
In this forested place
With its cold clean air
And long views
And low orange light

Always a bird flies against a window   Confused by reflections
Drops, at breakfast time, neck back
One drop of blood at its beak
These small cruel things

We rake up leaves into a pile
High enough for all of us
Bury ourselves in that smell
Of summer going back to earth
Two children, not mine, squealing
Running, my sister like an anchor now
Around which we swing at our moorings
Our ropes loose and long

The sheep in the warm sweet barn
Where someone has left the radio on
And an aria mixes with their sounds

...

It snows in the night
A soft, deep snow, piled along each twig & branch
Muffling the brook
Flattening our leaf pile

We watch our childhood repeating
The toys, the stories, the things they do
Not knowing that we did them once before
The same toboggan, the same books, the wooden blocks

Me beached across an ocean
My sister on another shore

A big land
A flat place crossed by a power line
The edge of town
A cold wind whistling through

The bees all Italian
Surprised to learn
That the Roman Empire still exists
Spread now to the Americas   even across the Americas
Still with ruthless hierarchies

Each small province with its workers
With its guards, its rigid paving
Its foray of discovery

...

1998

1 January   [Scanno]

Me, dazzled to be handling something
Precious as the stars,
Opening and opening this box of jewels

Arrows of time
Flying in all directions

We have come again to this high valley
This house by the lake
These blue winter skies

By four o'clock, the sun already gone
Behind the mountain at our back,
The ridge across golden just above Frattura
And reflecting in the water,
Almost touching our shore

A new year has begun
Tomorrow I am thirty-eight
And still striding up mountain paths
With the sun on the snow
And the cold air filling my lungs

And still prodding under my arms
My neck, my groin,
Hoping not to feel lumps

Yesterday we went to see Liborio,
Nudging along the icy road
Coming down into his valley,
To his basin of sunshine,
Found him by his barn, his huge hands and great hooked nose,
lamenting a sheep lost to a wolf, remembering all over again the years
in Montreal, in Beaconsfield, the French, De Gaulle, the tunnel, Expo
67 … Only this time I can understand it all, and at lunch, at a long
table by the fire, I am made an honorary Abbruzzese. And I would

come here too, to be old, like the women in black with their fine skin & their eternal, shining eyes. Going about the passageways & streets & squares like guardians of something secret & sublime, with a posture & a dignity as erect as mountains, clean as snow. I would be one of them. They shine like priestesses among the Roman women in their store-bought furs.

Coming down from the hills this afternoon we heard a flute across the little valley, something ancient, from some more eastern place, a handful of notes in a minor key. We saw sheep flowing along the hill-side, rivulets of sheep splitting & merging & splitting again, & pooling & flowing, their bells too in minor keys coming so clear across the cold, still air.

2 January

My thirty-eighth birthday. A disorganised day, waking up late, grey & cold. A walk up high, a coffee in Scanno. Saw a pig drawn up by its hind legs under a stout tree at the edge of town, head soaked in blood, a dozen men around sliding out its entrails, carving it up. Packed, drove back to Pescara, a simple supper, bath. Tired now. A few small lumps. Praying & praying that they'll stay away & let me get on with my life.

3 January

Brilliant warm sunshine, almost hot, pooling here against a white-washed wall. Impossible to imagine Cambridge dark & cold & grey. These days I would travel a long way for a few rays of sun.

It's a numbing kind of place, the constant stream of cars & people & food. The hours spent at the table, eating, talking, eating.

At Liborio's it seemed to me there is still a foreignness in the world. Still the possibility of difference. And how we might have crossed before Expo 67, the Italian pavilion with its reinforced concrete and its carabinieri. And now in the mountains, each abandoned house.

This mountain valley
Everywhere traces of the people who have left
These houses with their stone walls bulging here
And toppling there, still a vine climbing the back

And the small stony plots of earth
You wonder which pizzerias in America
Are run by the grandsons of the people who lived here

Which antique families became immigrants
The ladies of Scanno with their long black skirts
The long lines of children, almost holy.

Have intoxicated [*sic*] with too much food & wine, I sleep
The brain sleeps, circles like a water bug
Without diving

Looking through bags of old photos
Children on beaches, dancing, stylish women
In piazzas, we pass like photos, click, click
And we're gone. To some, children. To some, none.

...

14 February [San Valentino]

Today has been like May
We remember how it is to feel warm,
How we too open like buds
How fast this winter went
('We'll pay for this at Easter')
'Nothing good comes free'
I don't believe that
Coming home over Grantchester meadows
The sky pink,
The willows still naked along the river
The wind almost warm
But these times can't last.
In California, the rains have not passed.
What speaks to you most now?
Last month I was in Germany,
It was so grey, so cold, for three days
I didn't leave the manor
Where the taxi left me,
Where my room was three floors up
Its windows almost curtained by the dark cedars

Looking down across the lawns
To the far road, a cyclist passing, a walker, a car
(Cathy lived in this town, before her father died)
I rode here in a train, all along the grey Rhine,
The rain slanting,
The flat boats going up & down
In my compartment was a priest,
Though you'd never know

19 February

After a lecture on superstring theory
How language & sculpture interact in the mind
Dimensions curl up
Is there anything special about a string?
So that illuminating it
From another angle
You see projected on the wall a fox
And then a tree
And then a bird
And you know it's all one thing
But you don't know it's a hand
And has four fingers & a thumb
And knuckles that bend

All particles are waves in the field

We are only seeing things from different points of view
In certain limits a theory metamorphoses
Into another, and another
Space curving in on itself

What is a field?
...

5 May

Life *à la carte*, and why not, order it up

Not really understanding anything
Just skimping across the surface

Like going upstream on stepping stones
You don't really know the meaning of river.
Cold wet feet, a current against you
You might get there, but you haven't understood.

So many stones
Building a cairn on a mountain top
Where few will go
I lift & place my few stones
And the wind & snow might knock them down

My sureness falters
...

30 August

Desire Lines

Blood thinned, the air holding tight
Oxygen is responsible for our thoughts
The molecular structures of our ideas
The clear liquids dropping into my veins
Not seeming to think too much
About the value of my life
Not consumed with questions of whether
Because staying alive is hard enough
And staying happy is even harder
So if you can do it, or help someone else
A little bit, to stay alive, or happy
Then that's enough
So why are we made to question
The value of our lives

La vita é un pelo perso sotto il letto

These small cells
Lighting their fires
In the Aladdins caves
Of your bones

Sown in the red earth of marrow
To swell and bring life

Could our bones be like that
The big thigh bones
The heart
The cavern
The dance in a bear skin

Thin air, this blood
Still asking personal questions
Still prying into the private life of stars
The when & where & which encounters
What was transformed
What torn out and lost

6 September

Post, a day of hard rain,
A cure taking hold,
Restructured in the earth
Us on the ends of telephone lines
Can't question the meaning of life
Say what you think
What you would like to say,
To tell everyone before you go
What life was like when you were young
What the universe is like out there

What is dark matter?

Forced to acknowledge that what we see is only
A tiny fraction of what is there
Not content with what we can see,
We go searching for what we can't
Plunging spears into dark water
Hoping for a fish
Waving nets in thin air

Planets, white dwarfs, dark stars, particles
The universe is full of dust

Not much to say
Most already said

Desire lines would lead to where?
A hot seashore with soft sand & shells & calm blue water
To sparkle through like bubbles
A driftwood hut empty, waiting to shelter us
Already sculpted & smoothed

To a mountain meadow full of wild flowers
Abbruzzo before the wars, & especially the rebuilding
When we all got impatient & greedy
And far too rich and alone.

Sunday 13 September   [Pescara]

Substituting your kitchen with its linoleum
For the kitchen of my childhood
With its linoleum
And another mother, yours,
Busy at the stove
And different smells
And out the window, red roofs,
Not grey, not steaming chimneys,
But ochre walls, peeling in the sun
And the sound of other people's lives,
Their arguments, their television,
And the smells of their Sunday lunches
Spilling over the boundaries of houses
Where our neighbourhood was silent   silent as stone, and stern
And stern, and stone

In England we live without roots   Sunday sounds of ice-cream vans
Without people around our table   Playing *Greensleeves* and
Telling us of uncles & cousins   stopping mid-phrase, and
Small conspiracies between grandsons
                    & grandmothers   overhead the antique
                                       planes circling
Fig trees, as if your leaves could hide   droning like flies
The immodesty of your arching trunks
Totem poles of buttocks thighs & midriffs
Ruffs & dimples & labial folds
Your fruit swelling straight from a branch
Your leaves suggesting modesty
In false modesty, hiding nothing

Shameless fig tree
Some clutch of maidens, victims of a
Jealous god

...

After the First September Storm

Just the old men with their papers now
Raffia skirts of closed umbrellas
Ruffling in the wind
The turquoise sea in swells
The spray blown back
The first of autumn's shells
& seppia bones, & sea-tossed things,
The new collection,
Uncollected on the sand

Thursday 17 September

Yesterday walked to Francavilla
All along the beach.
Clear sky, turquoise sea
Calm as a bath at first
And swimming out a bit
You see inland the Majella
Covered already with a fresh
Fall of snow
Then walking & walking
And a wind comes up,
A south wind, a Garbino
Here there are names for all the winds
And walking & walking
Passing dead fish, a dead cat
Washed up, someone discreetly
Covered it with a board
Live fish too, like minnows,
And one that jumps when I'm out
Swimming, and small creeping things
And a flat kind of beetle walking
Hopelessly towards the water
And upended by every wave.

Now and then a jogger.
Two nuns in white
Old men, old ladies, bending,
Knee deep, collecting something
In the shallow water
Sometimes a mother & a daughter,
Old, strolling, talking.
And when we get back to
The port, the wind full up
And white caps out to sea
All the hairs along my arms
Standing up in goosebumps
In the September sun.
At home I sleep the late
Afternoon away, wake up
Thinking it must be late,
Already light, and we
Work in the garden a bit,
Pulling away canes & bindweed
From the eucalyptus & bamboo
That some day will bring
Privacy & life to this poor
Garden again.

...

[Tuesday] 22 September

Absolution
Just the sound of the bells signalling the start of mass
Might be enough to make you think that
A virtual absolution is as good as an actual one
Confessing to yourself is as good as kneeling in a darkened
                                                confessional
Whispering to a faceless priest who is only human
So that even before the bells stop clanging
Your slate of sin has been wiped clean
And you can begin again.
...

8? October   [Yorkshire]

Travelling North, direct towards the dipper
As if you might break through the eggshell
Of sky and find yourself with no meaning of north
No more than two stars somewhere
In the Milky Way might chance to line up
To point at our pole

The semblance of drifting through space
When we are really moving at 220k/s

Sheep, walls, stones with sky coming through

9 October

Me north as home, you south
Like a dog chasing a stick
Lapping along the high ridge
With the wind, against the wind
Fine rain from a clear sky
And a haze & rainbow at the
High top end to end in the vales
And dales, stone & walls
Small light through a mislaid stone
Lead crystals in a lump of slate
...

Transumanza

Always moving towards the easy place
The green grass
I should do that too
Drive my flock of self
Over the last high pass
Down to the lowlands
Why can't I do that too?
Drive myself down into the
Sweet meadows of the south
Knowing there will always be a spring
Instead of sticking it out in a high

Craggy place
In the thin cold air
As if it were enough to know
That you can go
And still come back

What if they tell me that my time is up
That I will never go again
Not even once
To the high peaks, to the seaside

And how in all this glory
Can it be a gene gone wrong
And why
And didn't my body know I needed it
For longer
That I haven't finished yet
And won't in six months
Or even years
Is there ever a time you're ready
To lay it down
To stop all the singing and dancing
To pass into what?

Is there any language, logic
Any algebra where death is not
The tragedy it seems
A geometry that makes it look
Alright to die
Where can it be proved
Some theorem
If P then Q and all is well
If not P then not Q either and all is gone
Or if not P then Q

Driving down the axes of your bones

12 November

And after all that
Cycling home through the dark streets
The homeless man with the penny whistle
Is playing your favourite tune
...

14 November 1998

Saturday's Child

Born too late for loving and giving,
Saturday's child must work for a living.

Born too soon for the Sabbath day,
Saturday's child has rent to pay.

Now, earning a living's not so bad,
Though just for one, it's a little sad.

So loving and giving as best she can,
Saturday's child found a man.

Married a Tuesday, full of grace,
(And unaccountably fair of face).

Both were open to a change,
Though a birthday's hard to rearrange.

A proper job can be quite taxing
If your talent is relaxing.

Equally, hell can be being idle:
Work is a horse that's hard to bridle.

Grace takes patience, Tuesdays know,
And Saturday's child has far to go.

The day you're born is the way you stay,
Whether it's fair, or blithe, or gay.

So Saturday's child's still up at eight,
While gracious Tuesday lies in late.

And Saturday dreams of a lazy age,
But, ever practical, earns her wage.

Telescopes   [Tenerife]

Those few brave pilgrims
Standing white robed
At the ~~boundary~~ edge
Of earth and sky
On their ~~dark~~ mountain
In the thin, ~~dark~~ dry air,
For all their altitude
No nearer, really, to the stars

But hopeful
And so patient, ~~tracking~~
High above the traffic
Of the lowlands, tracking
The minutiae of the Universe
Attentive to a different light.

---

22 November

Why is it that markets
Piled high with fruit & vegetables
Make you cry:
For all the terrible things we do
This earth keeps rewarding us
Keeps piling its treasures on our laps
Like a child that wants to be loved
Like something too trusting
That goes on wanting to be loved.

The old women with their kerchiefs
And their knuckled hands/fingers
Feeding strangers
Putting food on strangers' tables
Sitting down to this melon
Which grew beneath her watchful eye
Attentive to its needs

And keep on doing it
While the daughters marry
And the sons move to the city

...

27 December   [Swaffham Prior]

The English Walk/ Boxing Day

Thrashing
Slashing out into the descending dark   hawkliness
Across a fen
Along a dyke
The hawthorns threshing in the wind   thicket
Slick clay
The wind in the dog's fur   The bit that looks like Greece
The wind in your hair   The twisted hawthorns – olive
And tugging   trunks
The nettles, brambles whipping your   And how on a summer
                          knees
And darkness almost down   day the light comes
The most almost lucid pewter light   down through the
Lying in the puddles on the drove road   meeting branches
And your feet sticky in the dark sucking clay

This after all the tensions   The dark man stooping for the
Of families thrown together   crown of thorns
The once a year of rubbing up the wrong way   Guilt like a dark cloak
Difficult mothers, prickly daughters, sullen sons   Pillager of pain

All of it kept in, the right words
The tightly buttoned waistcoat, belt   How a dyke, a hedgerow,
                                  and a fen can be
Primrose No.1: as it is   a world, a life, a

Primrose No.2: sunset and a wedding ring
Primrose No.3: cosmic light

refuge, a temple

Like refugees fleeing from
the too-close parlours,
the disputed music, the
twitches and irritations

And then, at the least prompting
Leaping up to go out and walk
'The dog would like it'
For the sake of the dogs
                For the dogs' sake

false laughs & too
many, the glut of empty
words filling the rooms as
if they needed filling, as
if listening together weren't
as good as talking

Imitations of the pony club mums
Flying out across the fen
Into its infinitely absorbing sky

Like a night march
Survived the war, returning home

The stout man with the crown of thorns
In his thick hand
Hurrying away ahead

Past thicket, shrine and travellers' camp
All of it transformed

In a sudden gust
We are leaping up
To out and walk [*sic*]
For the dogs' sake
What is stifled
Left, we are out
Thrashing out across a fen
With darkness almost coming down
Out along a dyke
With thicket walls and roof
The wind hacking at the hawthorns
Brambles whipping up against your knees
Past the bit that looks like Greece
The twisted hawthorn-olive trees
The way in summer sunlight
clay
Filters through the leafy roof
How a fen, a dyke, a hedge
Can be world, temple, life.

Whipping out like dark ribbo
Swept up into the all absorbi
                sky
The dark man
With the crown of thorns
That wasn't his
In his thick hand
Hurrying ahead

This is a kind of fanning
Of a dark flame

Trudging in the dark
Our bootsoles sucking at the

Bowing down the cloister
Of a hawthorn arch

The liquid pewter light
Lying on the puddles
Of the drove road
Travellers' road
And your bootsoles sucking at the clay
Refugees of Christmas parlours.
Fleeing through the night
Each one's irritations
Each one's
All the difficult mothers
Prickly daughters
Sullen sons

...

1999

Sunday 31 January 1999

... The false starts
That line your green veins with bruise

...

In Me Now

In me now
Are traces of the Madagascar periwinkle
Mustard gas
And mutant genes
And things made inside mice
Marked cells
And strangers' blood
And something iridescent in the lymph
Like in the spines of fish
That filter phosphorescence
From the sea

Inventory

Two scars are pink, one white
Where flesh was taken
Three small tube holes underneath
A collar bone
Two slits on tops of feet
A tiny dot tattoo for lining up the lungs
A cluster of white puncture marks
On each knob of hip-backbone
Where cores come out, and aspirate
And all the little needle nicks
Soft inside the elbow-skin
...

1 February 1999

Symptoms

Blood roaring in your ears
Like the sea
Heart thumping fast like at altitude
But no crest, no summit, no view

Nausea, swollen feet
Like pregnancy
But no child.
...

28 February

First sun for months, it seems
Warm & bright
Frogs mating, one on the back of the other
For hours
Planted seeds

Who will I have been
When I'm gone

Violation of the body
The little crowd of strangers
Who have taken my body
With needles and knives
And then gone home
To watch TV
And the bits of me, stashed
Away in freezers
A kind of immortality

There is no poetry to cancer
To the body betraying itself
Ravishing itself
Leaving itself drained

...

6 March

A child is like a clock
Resets your own sense of time

Poem for M.'s eightieth birthday

    So much a secret kind of life
    For me more imagined than known
    Except as mother
    Making sandwiches for school lunches
    For picnics at St Hilaire
    The brown paper bag, the apple
    No fuss.

This image: legs crossed, one under, one free
        on the sofa
        sun streaming in
        New Yorker rolled open
        reading
...

Born in the wrong generation
To be twenty when the war began
And the men began to die
Europe a place of danger
And the red-haired man?
Picking edelweiss on an alp?
And marrying late, late for then,
Of all people to my father

Of all people to be born
But me, and have a life
And leave
Do I want to write it all down?

...

29 April

Who would have thought
I'd be the first to go
Of all of us
The first departure
First death
And ten years to contemplate
The going
Why me to face all this?

Can't I just go back
To the mountains
To the lakes & rivers

But first, I want to restring
All your beads
The ones that snapped and spilled
In trains
And found their way home
To jam jars

Monday 3 May

In the garden of greens and shade
Of a May fresh from April
One foot already in June,
Impatient to explore each last possibility
Of green from the blue lavender,
To the quintessential cherry
To the yellowing, drying fritillaries
Whose day came back in March.
Impatient to say all these greens
Before the flowers begin to chatter,
To become loud with colour,
To let themselves go lewdly and loudly
Into scarlets, purples, & indigos.

From Stones to Stars

1ole system 'vibrates', as kinet
/erted back to kinetic energy, a
l theorem,

$$\frac{1}{2}\frac{d^2 I}{dt^2} = 2T + W$$

is the kinetic energy, and W is

$$t_{vr} \approx 3/[4(2\pi G\rho_m)^1$$

nsity ρ_m in units of $M_\odot$ pc^{-3},

$$t_{vr} \approx 4.5 \times 10^6 \rho_m^{-1/2}$$

(2.2) we can write

$$t_{vr} \approx 0.2 t_{cross}.$$

year old LMC clusters will prob
/ young objects like the central

Every year of my childhood, on the day in June that school let out, my sister and I were bundled into the family camper van, and the long voyage westward began: our summer holiday and my father's season of field work. For three months we would roam around northern Canada exploring the shores of a huge prehistoric lake, Lake Agassiz, which drained into Hudson's Bay 8,000 years ago, leaving behind Lake Winnipeg and Lake Manitoba as the biggest of its remnants. Often we didn't arrive back in Montreal until mid-September, returning to school a week or two late with apologetic notes from our parents.

It was certainly on these voyages that my scientific education began. Almost more than an education, it was a natural process of assimilation, like a child learning to speak her native tongue. My father's field work, at least the part I knew most about, was to trace the evolution of Lake Agassiz's shores. We would criss-cross the prairies and spruce forests of Ontario, Manitoba and Saskatchewan, looking for prehistoric beaches: ridges of sand and gravel overgrown with grasses, sweet clover, black spruce. When we found one we would stop and my father would fill a small sample bag with limestone pebbles. I could help with this, as picking up stones came naturally. Even as a five- or six-year-old, my eye was trained to distinguish a limestone pebble from a sandstone one or a piece of chert. I would poke the pebbles through a square grid cut by my father in the bottom of a plastic box, to standardise their size, and then judge their roundness on a scale from one to ten. Number one was rough and jagged. Ten was as perfect as a marble. From the average roundness of pebbles on a particular beach, my father could deduce how long the waves had washed against that shore. It was a long time before I realised that to most people, beaches were where you went to swim.

I was also put to use as scale in photographs, standing atop ancient end moraines, beside exposed varves in banks of clay, in front of synclines and anticlines, or once, when our travels took us as far west as the Canadian Rockies, knee deep in mud at the mouth of a living, breathing glacier. In Sudbury, Ontario, where pollution from nickel mining had stripped the land of all vegetation, and the surface-of-the-moon landscape was ideal for studying erosion, I was sent to scout out examples of the concentric crescent shaped cracks in outcrops of bedrock that showed that a glacier had passed there, and in which direction it was moving. (The marks were the same as you got by dragging your spoon across the smooth flat surface of a bowl of jelly – one of the few occasions where playing with food was tolerated in the name of science.)

I also collected pebbles of my own, as many as were allowed, the quota being set by my father's fear of overloading the van's suspension. They were not limestone but mottled granite, shiny black obsidian, flint, fossils, pumice. I also collected birch bark and birds' nests, shells and small animal bones. Back home I labelled things and set up exhibitions in the playroom, some of which became part of show-and-tell projects at school, and have been respectfully preserved to this day.

The experimenting didn't end with the summer. In autumn, with the first hard frosts, parts of our little city garden became off bounds, as my father measured and photographed the needle ice pushing up the soil between my mother's dying flowers. There was a year when we traced the path of the sun through the seasons by making a kind of sundial. My father taped a small square of cardboard with a hole punched in it to a window which looked south across the city towards the St Lawrence river. Once a week at noon we made a pencil mark where the sunlight streaming through the hole struck the wall opposite. As the months passed an arc began to take shape as the noon sun first dipped low in the sky, and then, as spring came, began to climb higher again.

One winter, when the snow came, my father and I collected snowflakes on a black velvet cloth. With a thin glass rod we picked them up and transferred them to microscope slides where a drop of some clear liquid (from a bottle labelled 'poisonous' that lived alongside soil samples in my mother's freezer) preserved their exact shapes, to look at under a microscope. I loved their beauty and complexity. And the shapes, my father explained, told you about the temperature high above, where the snowflakes crystallised, and about what they encountered as they floated downwards.

With all this, geology never seemed to me so much a career, as something to do on weekends and summer holidays with my father, and it never really occurred to me to actually study it. As a child and as a young adult I had three or four interests and corresponding heroes of my own. One was Jane Goodall: I longed to go to Africa to live among the chimpanzees. One was Louis Leakey and the million-year-old fossil hominids he and his family were unearthing in Kenya's Rift Valley. During the summers I would be Leakey, excavating in the Canadian north for ancient bones (and finding flint tools which, if not millions of years old, were in a few cases at least thousands). A third fascination was the Galapagos Islands and their exotic fauna, introduced to me by Jacques Cousteau. It was never the facts that interested me so much as the possibilities they opened up to the imagination. What I did to entertain myself during the long summer days in the back of the camper van, crossing forests and prairies, was to write poems.

My childhood coincided with the most ground-breaking years of space exploration. I clearly remember the sight, in the summer of my ninth year, of astronauts climbing down their ladder to the surface of the moon. Our big square bakelite television was specially moved for the occasion from the playroom to the dining room, where the reception was better. But the excitement surrounding the event was more my mother's than my own. I didn't really understand that going to the moon was difficult or new. It all seemed mechanical and remote, and the moon itself, colourless and a bit bleak.

The night sky, on the other hand, was a place where one's imagination could expand infinitely. The skies of northern Canada were dazzling, and lying on my back I used to hope that if I stared hard enough at one star, so that the others seemed to fade from view, then whatever beings lived there might transmit images of themselves and their world. Even the little square of starless sky outside my city bedroom window was a fertile field, and as an eight- or nine-year-old I used to lie awake after bedtime wondering what it meant for the Universe to be infinite, and what might be out there.

Science was also, of course, part of my formal education, though my memories of this are less pleasurable. Rarely was school science an opportunity for real exploration. One occasion, when I was about eight, was a simple experiment where we were asked to mix together earth, water, and salt, and then separate them. We had available a coffee-filter and a candle flame, but no one told us that we first had to filter out the dirt, and then evaporate the water over the candle. Finding this solution all by myself was exhilarating. For the most part school science was textbook learning: memorising names and arrangements of human organs or plant parts. Experiments were essentially like following recipes, trying to make the results come out the way you knew they were supposed to. The subject may have been science, but the process wasn't.

When I finished high school, I went away to college in the United States, a possibility introduced by my New England mother and Yale educated father. (As a small child I had never quite understood the distinction between Yale and jail, and the fact that my father had spent time there in the years before I was born was perplexing.) On the encouragement of a close family friend and alumna of the college, I chose Smith. I went with the idea of majoring in Biology or English, but quickly decided that I could write without having to major in English. Genetics had been a late high school fascination, so alongside the Galapagos Islands and chimpanzees, Biology seemed a good choice. In the end, I never took a single course in that department. One evening in my second semester a friend and housemate Neville (also a geologist's daughter) came back describing her Astronomy 101 class, and I knew instantly that I was missing something. The very next term I signed up.

The Smith Astronomy Department was run by three faculty members: Mr White, who taught most of my classes; Ms Seitter, who spent half of each year in Germany; and Mrs J., who helped out in the labs. (The J. stood for an unpronounceable Polish name.) Ms Seitter and Mrs J. together had a kind of old world, big-bosomed warmth, and a ready sense of celebration. They would gather us around them for afternoon discussions with endless cups of coffee and special cookies Ms Seitter brought back with her from Germany. They would rout us out of our little student office late at night, squeeze us all into Ms Seitter's white VW bug and take us downtown for ice cream. Between the three of them, and the new kinds of questions I had never even thought before to ask, astronomy soon became the obvious choice of major.

I still remember clearly the week we learned about the Hertzsprung-Russell diagram. We were given a list of brightnesses and colours for stars in a globular cluster: one of about two hundred spherical swarms of stars, all the same age, that drift around in the halo of our Galaxy. Our task was to plot the brightnesses against the colours. As if by magic, a pattern emerged. Rather than a scatter plot, all the stars swept out a sinuous path on the graph paper. The Hertzsprung-Russell diagram which we had 'discovered' is perhaps the most important diagnostic tool used by astronomers to assess the evolutionary state of a system of resolved stars, and remains at the heart of my research today.

I also remember the nights on the roof of the science centre, learning how to find objects with the little telescope. The clearest nights were always the coldest ones, and the pleasure of looking at planets and nearby nebulae was tempered by freezing fingers and toes. And scuffling across the carpeted floor of the telescope dome would cause a build-up of static electricity which discharged as a painful spark when you set your eye against the brass eyepiece. There were better moments too, and one which stands out is a trip to the bigger sixteen-inch telescope at nearby Whately, during which I saw for the first time our sister galaxy, Andromeda. It gave an almost vertiginous feeling to see this delicate wisp of milky spiral light floating in what seemed a bottomless well of empty space.

I spent my junior year abroad at St Andrews University in Scotland. In a letter he sent me towards the end of my stay, Mr White suggested that I look into applying to work as a research student at the Royal Observatory in Edinburgh the summer after. I did so, and it was perhaps one of the most influential experiences in my ultimate choice of astronomy as a career. I was set to work in the plate library up on Blackford Hill, overlooking the sparkling blue water of the Firth of Forth, scanning the Universe, searching for elliptical galaxies with dust lanes.

Every inch of the northern hemisphere sky was photographed in the 1950s and 1960s using the Schmidt telescope at Mt Palomar in California. The plates, 935 of them altogether, were about fourteen inches on a side, and an eighth of an inch thick. They were kept in thick brown envelopes, stacked vertically in grey metal cabinets. One by one, I lifted them out by their edges, nervous of breaking them, and slipped them into a frame on top of a big light table. Then I scanned them by eye, back and forth in one-inch strips, looking for a particular kind of galaxy: smooth and elliptical in shape, but bisected by an opaque lane of dust. The plates are negatives, so the dust lanes showed up white against the black of starlight. When I finished with the northern hemisphere I moved onto the south, which was still being photographed at the time with a telescope in Australia, on nerve-wrackingly thin glass plates that had to bend to be positioned at the telescope's prime focus.

The galaxies in question were peculiar in that ellipticals were supposed to be ancient systems: just stars, no gas or dust that might indicate recent star formation. Identifying a sample of these for future studies would help reveal how galaxies formed. In all I found forty of them, and was second author on an article published in the *Monthly Notices of the Royal Astronomical Society*, the main UK astronomy journal. Despite the rarity of these galaxies, scanning the plates never got boring. It was like lying on my back staring at the night sky. My mind could wander over all the questions of space and infinity and origins that I had always loved to think about. And the galaxies, in all their different forms, the wisps, the bars, the spirals, the smooth ellipses, each one different from the next, reminded me of nothing so much as the snowflakes my father and I had caught and preserved on glass those winter afternoons.

Physics was a problem. To pursue astronomy, I would have to study physics. Mathematics was fine. It had always been enjoyable and, (or because), I had always been blessed with good teachers. But physics had always seemed dull: batteries, light bulbs, billiard balls, rigid laws, the power to predict where a cannon ball might land, to manipulate the world. I got no joy from these powers. And to make matters worse, the technique frequently used to spice things up was to build up a certain common sense expectation about an experiment, and surprise the students with a counterintuitive outcome. I learned not to trust my intuition.

By my final year at Smith I knew I wanted to go on to the next step in an astronomy career, a Ph.D. I also wanted to return to Britain, partly because I had found an affinity with its culture, and partly to escape the barrage of exams that form part of a North American Ph.D. programme. But I wouldn't be accepted in a British Ph.D. programme in astronomy without a bit more background in physics, so I set off for the University of British Columbia to do a Master's degree in physics.

It was a daunting experience. My meagre Smith background in physics had at least been acquired in a supportive environment. Of the two hundred or so students in my freshman physics class, all were women. At UBC I repeatedly found myself in classes and seminars where I was the only woman. Often it felt like walking into the men's bathroom by mistake. The course work was overwhelming because my background was woefully inadequate. It was a struggle just to stay afloat. I remember months of rain and early morning lectures in statistical mechanics where, week after week we laboured at solving a complicated differential equation in order to understand why a bubble floating around a room will tend to want to attach itself to a wall, and from there slip over to where two walls meet, and finally slide up into a corner, which it will never leave. There were, however, two pleasures: quantum mechanics, which presented intriguing paradoxes, and general relativity, which let the imagination wander the same way the dark space outside my bedroom window had, probably because it was itself something geometrical, a language for exploring space.

In the second year, my scholarship was withdrawn because my grades didn't measure up, and the head of the department called me into his office and suggested that not everyone was cut out for this kind of thing, and perhaps I should reassess my goals. I continued, supporting myself as a lab assistant, and was lucky enough to find a friend, an ex-St Andrews student studying quantum gravity, who helped me along and bolstered my confidence. Also, I had by then applied to the Ph.D. program at Cambridge University, and had a letter from the director offering me a place. The best strategy seemed to be to move on as quickly as possible, leaving the demoralising atmosphere of UBC behind.

The subject of my Master's thesis was dynamical friction. Much as friction will cause a book pushed across a table to slow down, so gravity can exert a drag on celestial bodies. The Earth will eventually spiral closer and closer to the Sun for this reason. In the mathematical expression for this effect there is a term which, as you consider the pull of more and more distant objects, becomes infinite. I was supposed to think about what this really meant. I didn't get very far with understanding this infinity, but did manage to produce a coherent discussion of various ways of formulating dynamical friction based on different kinds of physics. It wasn't an original piece of research, but it was a useful exercise in learning to survey the scientific literature and bring different approaches to bear on a single problem. Two years after my arrival, almost to the day, I went to my supervisor with my Master's thesis in one hand, and a plane ticket to London in the other. The thesis was accepted, though somewhat grudgingly, and that autumn I began my Ph.D. in Cambridge.

The first few months in Cambridge were a mixture of excitement and nervousness at being in a place so full of history and prestige, and a sense of confusion over reconciling my rather abstract interest in quantum mechanics and general relativity with the reality that my background had prepared me for a more pragmatic kind of research. On a late autumn afternoon Mike Fall, who was to become my thesis supervisor, spread out on his desk in front of me photographs of dense star clusters in the Large Magellanic Cloud, our nearest neighbour galaxy. This galaxy, he explained, contained a unique population of clusters: rich in stars like the ancient clusters in the halo of our own Galaxy, but some of them very young. Why was the Large Magellanic Cloud still forming massive clusters where our own Galaxy had ceased to billions of years ago? What could we learn from these objects about the way rich star clusters form? The questions seemed interesting and I set out to learn more.

The following autumn Mike called me into his office to introduce a colleague visiting from Australia, Ken Freeman. He told me he had decided to spend a six month sabbatical in California, and proposed that I spend the six months at Mount Stromlo Observatory near Canberra, Australia, working with Ken, learning to observe with large telescopes, and collecting data on the Large Magellanic Cloud clusters. (The Large Magellanic Cloud is only visible from the southern hemisphere during the southern summer, a happy circumstance which provided many occasions to escape from the dreary English winters.)

At Mount Stromlo I lived in a house at the base of the hill where the astronomy department and local telescopes were situated. I often went for walks down a sandy road into a valley behind the house where, at dusk, the distant gum-tree covered hills turned a deep blue, and groups of kangaroos would startle and bound away at my approach. At night, with no city lights nearby, the sky was dazzling; even more so than the skies of northern Canada, because the southern sky has the lion's share of bright objects. While our northern Milky

Way arches away into the hinterland of the Galaxy, the southern Milky Way plunges straight into the Galaxy's turbulent centre. For the first time I saw the Large Magellanic Cloud itself, a full-moon-sized patch of pale light that looked like a fragment torn out of the Milky Way.

In the mid-1980s astronomy was in a period of transition. Computers were turning from specialized instruments into ubiquitous tools, and the technology was changing rapidly. In my first computing course at Smith we had learned how to program with punch cards. By the time I began my Ph.D., punch cards had become relics of a past age. Technology for gathering data was also changing rapidly, as sensitised photographic plates were being replaced with electronic detectors whose output could be displayed and manipulated directly with computers.

Thus, part of my time at Mount Stromlo was spent in a basement room counting stars on photographic plates in order to determine the structure of the star clusters I was studying, and part was spent at the telescopes both at Mount Stromlo and at the large international observatory in the outback 500 miles north, collecting data electronically. I loved observing. I loved the moment at sunset when all the domes would glow orange-pink, and one by one their shutters would open as the observers began their preparations for the night. I loved the way the wind would come up in the night and fill the dark dome, which rattled like rigging, the stars sailing dizzyingly overhead.

By the time I returned to Cambridge the following summer, Mike had decided to leave to take up a position at the headquarters of the Hubble Space Telescope Institute in Baltimore, Maryland. Not wishing to lose the continuity of my thesis project, I opted to remain his student, and spent several extended periods in Baltimore. It was exciting to move around and see new places, but there were also lonely times, moving again and again to new places where I knew no one. Still, the Space Telescope Institute was a bustling place with the Hubble telescope about to be launched, and it was a good opportunity to get to know, and be known in, the astronomy community.

All in all my Ph.D. went smoothly along, and three and a half years after arriving in Cambridge (the standard allotment for a British Ph.D.) I delivered my thesis to the Board of Graduate Studies, and processed through the ancient Senate House to kneel at the Chancellor's feet, be doffed on the head and pronounced, in Latin, Doctor of Philosophy with all the rights and privileges thereof. My years in Cambridge had brought none of the struggle and alienation of UBC, and I felt excited at the prospect of my next move, to take up a postdoctoral research fellowship at the Institute for Advanced Studies in Princeton, New Jersey.

Despite what one might imagine, the Institute of Astronomy in Cambridge had never really seemed a bastion of male scientists, at least not the way the Institute for Advanced Studies in Princeton turned out to be. Of course Cambridge was dominated by men, but apart from a few irksome details (male graduate students were listed by their initials, females were required to list their titles, either Miss or Mrs) that didn't seem to matter. Princeton on the other hand was irrefutably male, both in the occupants of E-building, where the astronomers worked, and in the way the place was run. In indefinable ways it was alienating. Jokes were made about the female sex. If one didn't laugh one 'didn't have much of a sense of humour'. The only path seemed to be to become bitter and embattled. I preferred to lie low in my office.

The situation was made worse by the explosion of the space shuttle Challenger in January 1986, eight months before I arrived in Princeton. I had been in Baltimore at the time, and remember the stunned silence in the auditorium where the staff had gathered to watch the shuttle launch on the large screen, and saw instead Challenger cascading Earthwards in ribbons of flame. With the disaster, the launch of the Hubble Space Telescope was delayed, and my reason for going to Princeton, to work with Hubble data, vanished. I found myself in a stronghold not just of men, but of theoreticians, who traditionally hold themselves above observers. Complicated equations would be solved on blackboards, chalk dust flying, in much the way other species might beat their chests or erect gaudy plumage. I withdrew. After three years in Princeton, my career was at a low ebb. The mismatch between my needs and the place had prevented me from forming any real collaborations, and that is a crucial step in becoming integrated into the research community and striking out as a fully-fledged researcher.

The saving grace of Princeton was a lively co-operative of poets. We met Tuesday evenings, often in my little apartment opposite the Institute, and read and discussed our poems. The contrast between these evenings and the famous Princeton Tuesday lunches, was striking. At the lunches, a sort of high table, made up of the permanent research staff and whichever postdocs were courageous and aggressive enough to claim places, would lead the interrogation of new postdocs and visitors, who were expected, essentially, to demonstrate that they were worthy members of the clique. On more than one occasion results from other institutions were referred to patronisingly as 'amusing little things'. The poets were far more expansive and congenial, and I enjoyed those evenings immensely. However, the discussions there were also a reminder that, although I loved the unlimited licence to invent, I also loved the sense of exploring not an inner, but an outer world, that was really there, in some objective sense.

After three years in Princeton, my next step was the Bunting Institute at Radcliffe, a kind of Institute for Advanced Studies for women. The atmosphere could not have been more different. All kinds of pursuits (even raising children!) were considered worthy, and the fellows (at all stages in their careers) talked to one another without the barriers imposed by rank. I found myself opening up, relaxing, and reassessing my subject in light of other people's views of it. People are almost always interested in astronomy. Being introduced, for instance, at parties as an astronomer gives you much better prospects for conversation than being introduced as a mathematician or a physicist. I felt appreciated as a kind of entertainer in the midst of a crowd pursuing serious real-life projects to do with politics, poverty, the status of women.

However, scientists at the Bunting needed independent affiliations with a local lab, and establishing such a relationship with Harvard's Center for Astrophysics up the street proved difficult. They felt that since they had not themselves chosen me, they weren't enthusiastic about supplying the resources of an office and computing facilities. The colleague who came to my rescue, Bill Press, was a member of staff at the Center for Astrophysics whom I had met through his frequent visits to Princeton. Like most of the senior men who have stepped in as mentors for me at crucial moments, he was the father of a daughter.

By the time my Bunting year finished I was so disenchanted with astronomy, and so far from a world like that of Ms Seitter and Mrs J., that I contemplated quitting (not for the first time, but for the most serious time). I applied for a job teaching in the Harvard Expository Writing programme. There was one last possibility: a postdoctoral position back in the other Cambridge, working with the about to be launched (four years late) Hubble Space Telescope. The day after I accepted the Expository Writing job, an offer came through to return as a postdoc to Cambridge. I taught for a term at Harvard, a valuable experience, which brought me into contact with a very different crowd. (Staff meetings included such things as readings from novels-in-progress.) Then I returned to Cambridge in the early spring.

Over the years that followed I finally began to find my voice, to feel at ease in the astronomy community, to feel appreciated for who I was, without having to put up façades and pretences. The Hubble Space Telescope was launched in April 1990 amidst great excitement, and then disappointment at the discovery that the mirror had been ground to the wrong shape and was unfocussable. Astronomers using the telescope persevered, applying fancy mathematical algorithms to sharpen up the images (the same technique as might be applied to sharpen up a photo of the licence plate of a distant speeding car). Even with the focus problem, the detail in the images was stunning compared to what was possible from the ground. In 1993 a mission was sent into orbit to install a set of lenses in the telescope to compensate for the distorted optics, and the tedious image processing was no longer necessary. I used the images the telescope was sending back to study the structure and stellar content of our Galaxy, of the Large Magellanic Cloud and its star clusters, and of distant galaxies, presenting the results at conferences in both Europe and North America, and initiating collaborations with people with whom it was a joy to work.

There are times when the enterprise seems mechanical, when the constraint to pursue the truth seems to suffocate the imagination, and the mysteries of the Universe seem irrelevant to the lives we humans lead down here. But on the whole, understanding the Universe seems a fundamental step in understanding our origins, and in establishing a sense of perspective with respect to space and time that I find comforting. Someone once said to me 'astronomy is like a big circus tent – there's room for everyone.' I feel privileged indeed to be able to spend my days inside a tent with such a dazzling roof.

Cambridge, England, May 1998